ISBN 978-0-6459740-1-0

1st Edition (b)e

© Jonas Hjertquist 2023

All rights reserved. No part of this book may be reproduced without the written consent of the author, Jonas Hjertquist.

Please note that the contents of this book are written for the expressed purposes of 1. Entertainment, and 2. Raising questions.

Under **no** circumstances should the views expressed in this book be assumed to represent the actual views of the author, publisher, editor or any other contributor.

Foreword   **1st Edition September 2023**

Just like the gag reflex can save your life, this book can do the same and just like the gag reflex you just don't know that it's needed until it really IS needed. It may come as a surprise, but in the world of words, their meanings and interpretations are changing rapidly, and you should now comfortably assume that you are, along with everybody else, gradually becoming an idiot.

Perhaps you are still unaware and think you are special, but slowly you are accepting all the idiocy around you. Perhaps you think it is a sign of intelligence to resist. But in thinking that you are hitting the nail on the head, you are 'thinking'...and this is a problem. It is much more rewarding, safe, and inclusive to abstain from thinking. Realise instead that it is only a matter of time until you too must join the ranks of idiots. It is inevitable.

Written by aspiring idiots who specialise in not very much, this slim volume shows anyone how to embrace the moron within. As budding imbeciles and cretins we must learn what to say and unlearn what not to say so that we may aspire to new levels of inertia and low brow lunacy as the greatest approach to life. This is the true recipe for long lasting happiness.

The Idiot's Guide to Idiots is a small dictionary representing a genuine attempt to elucidate the reader on terms which often are undergoing radical transformation from previously established dictionary definitions.

We must embrace the comforting and inevitable societal change into a utopian world of leisure, narcissistic fulfilment, gluttony, gaming, daytime soaps, and other important things.

If you want to be a hapless lummox or want to unlearn how to find the doorknob **THE IDIOT'S GUIDE TO IDIOTS** is for you.

On the other hand, in the unlikely event you don't think you are quite ready to join the growing ranks of foolish idiots around you, this is the perfect guide to seeing the world as it is seen by dullards, without restraining the English language with archaic notions of tradition, convention or reality. In the final analysis this A to Z guide is a warm invitation to join the well-established and fast-growing universe of whimsical, wilful ignorance and boisterous buffoonery.

"Everything is changing. People are taking their comedians seriously and the politicians as a joke."   Will Rogers.

Why would you want to be different anyway? It is risky and fraught with danger to be different or to stand out.

A zebra without stripes is first to die. To be different also runs opposite to human nature. We want to be part of the collective and join in something bigger than ourselves and the biggest group of all is, you guessed it, idiots.

You are aware of this. Most people around you are idiots already. You know it because you see it every day. A peculiar observation we have made is that the greater the distance from you, the bigger idiots people tend to be. The biggest idiots of all are to be found in other lands, other cultures and in politics. This is a universal truth that somehow can't be explained. Not by an idiot anyway.

We say this, not to divide us, because at the end of the day, we, all of us have this in common. We really are feeble minded fools, every single one of us, or soon we will be. Most books demonstrate this in a million ways, which is why they are best avoided, but the easiest way to confirm this fact is just to turn on the television or look at your social media feed. You will see an endless parade of idiots doing and saying the most dull-witted things imaginable, and still, we listen to them, look up to them and often emulate and even imitate them.

It is also important to recognise the difference between an idiot and an asshole. Idiots are dull-witted and slow but in no way are they self-serving and intentionally disrespectful in their conduct to others, the way that assholes are. Idiots may fumble and fail but they will not push, cheat, or shout. An idiot just likes to relax and chill out and an idiot wants you to join in.

So, we offer our congratulations to you for buying this book so that you may immerse yourself in words and their evolving interpretations and meanings. Many words will surprise, and some may upset, but all the while remember that the authors are idiots too.

In these pages you will receive the tools to literally show everyone that you are an idiot to be reckoned with and that you can beat anyone at this game.

The odd person, the really odd person, may choose to consider it offensive to be called an idiot but, you may take great comfort in the knowledge that you are in the presence of a true idiot. Possibly a little unaware (stupid) but certainly a fool of note. The only other possibility is that you have met the biggest asshole in the room.

Each word is carefully chosen, and we treat it as follows; first you will get a description of its traditional, often outdated *dictionary interpretation*, then we may reveal actual, more correct interpretations, or at least illustrate how the word can be used or abused, and occasionally we will eviscerate (*lit. to empty a chicken*) those that think it appropriate to perpetrate such abuse. And we cannot be politically correct, instead we wish to provide you with an arsenal of sarcastic and idiotic tools to reject anything you don't agree with and laugh pomposity and narcissistic, educated insolence in the face. This is the new and improved English language. Embrace it. Not that you have a choice. Change is coming.

There you have it. A short introduction so that you may delve, headfirst, into the evolution of the English language, especially as championed by those who stand to gain most out of the utopia that is sure to follow; journalists, social justice warriors, social media executives, speech writers, language moderators and politicians all around us.

We welcome your involvement as the second edition will contain many more words and feel free to make suggestions by emailing the author directly at hjertquist@gmail.com.
All new and original contributions or improvements to existing entries will be printed in the next edition and will be credited to you.
I.E., your name will be in print as a contributor.

Disclaimer.
We apologise for the correct spelling of words. According to some universities it is increasingly considered 'white, male and elitist' to do so. This is unintentional and as idiots we will not take responsibility for those who imagine this will represent the collapse of the linguistic traditions of the previously confusing and ineffective English language.

Any ridicule, anger or disappointment, real or imagined, in the contents of this modest volume should properly be directed at those intellectually sluggish, thoughtless troglodytes who publicly abuse and belittle language even more than we do.

Jonas Hjertquist Oct 2023

We dedicate this idiotic book of words
to the legendary wordsmith George Carlin.
If only he knew the buffoonery he is missing.

𝒜 - 49

Aardvark
A sub-Saharan animal with a long snout.
Usually thought of as the first word in a dictionary but as any idiot knows the first word is 'dictionary'. But it's a start.

Abandon
To withdraw completely, discontinue or desert.
We are said to have abandoned reason for madness.
But we clearly are not all mad. We are idiots. As idiots we know that we should abandon the archaic concept of critical thinking. It turns out language and reason are hardly worth a cent and just like a cent, not to be taken too seriously.
When abandoning a ship, the captain should be the last to leave. However, one Italian captain has famously abandoned this tradition.

Ability
Power, capacity, or competence to act.
The ability to act or do something, like running, doesn't mean you will win a marathon or even be passably co-ordinated. Ability is marginally more useful than inability but that is all. An ability to speak doesn't mean you have anything of value to say. However, do not permit such negativity to interfere with your right to speak your mind. Remember, it isn't what you say that matters. It is that you can say it.

Able
Empowered, qualified, or authorised.
If you are able to do something that doesn't mean you should. Clearly, being 'able' is the first step towards something that is supposed to be subjectively meaningful. For example, an ability to argue coherently might mean you can avoid paying some of your taxes. But why would you? Idiots like paying taxes.

Abolish
To put an end to or do away with.
Christian abolitionists were among the first and most vocal opponents of slavery and they acted to put an end to this immoral trade. Since we no longer have any Christian abolitionists there is no slavery. Likewise, we must abolish the police because then we will not have any crime. This is completely logical. We should abolish money too, then there would be no pay gap or poverty.
In fact, poverty itself should be abolished. That will work.

Abracadabra
A mystical word or magical expression often used to ward off misfortune, harm, or illness.

Some magic can be bought on the street corner and other magic happens when dropping your toast but without saying abracadabra neither ends well.

Absent
Not where you should be, or non-existent.
Being absent may mean that you miss something, like an appointment or perhaps an epiphany or original thought, but in most cases, being absent is a useful strategy and a means to avoid taking responsibility for decisions made while you were suffering a severe case of Munchausen syndrome.

Absolute
Free from imperfection, complete, perfect.
Being wrong is not as wrong as being absolutely wrong. This word, 'absolutely', supercharges language and provides additional emphasis to anything at all. It is actually used so much these days that if you don't use it people may not believe you. So, simply 'being wrong' and not 'absolutely wrong', is suddenly not wrong at all.
That's right, isn't it? Not absolutely right, but right.

Abstinence
Self-restraint or self-denial of appetites or alcohol.
Among many negative outcomes, abstinence causes lucid thinking. Abstinence is also the reason for lucid thinking. Thus, among human concepts, abstinence is both the cause and effect of itself. Effective catalysts to bring about this confusing outcome are taking ice baths, sitting in the lotus position on top of a pillar or abstaining from abstinence itself. Raw garlic is less effective.

Abstruse
Hard to understand.
Here then is further evidence that you and everyone you know is an idiot. This word, meaning hard to understand is, in of itself, hard to understand. Surely that could not have been the intent, but the irrefutable fact is that it is hard to understand.

Account
An oral or written description or narrative. Also, where your bank claims your money is.
A bank account is best kept secret from everyone, including yourself. Nobody wants to see all the money they don't have. Also, not being able to account for the empty account can be very upsetting.

Accountability
Liable or answerable for words or actions.
Taking responsibility for anything is totally unnecessary. Instead, claim victimhood. We can all do that in order to plausibly avoid taking

responsibility. Media and Prosecutors are uninterested in pursuing criminals as they prefer treating them as victims of social inequities. In this way the government has essentially abolished crimes like murder and assault so they can refocus on serious crime, like hate speech or trespassing on your own property.

Accounting
A system for maintaining and analysing the financial status of a company or individual.
An accountant is very useful for solving problems nobody knows they have in a way that nobody understands.
Etymologically the word has evolved from a-count-ant = A busy aristocrat, diminutive in stature (Presumably familiar with rudimentary arithmetic).

Acronym
A word formed from the initial letters from words in a set phrase.
This is the perfect word to illustrate how idiotic we have all become. Nearly everyone thinks an acronym is the same as an abbreviation. It is not. An acronym can be pronounced as a word, like NASA or SCUBA. So, CIA is not an acronym, it is an agency of hyperintelligence.

Acting
The art, profession, or act of performing fictional roles in real life, onstage or on screen.
Everybody acts. We act up, act stupid, act innocent, act crazy, act silly. Notice the theme? We seem to justify negative behaviour by pretending it isn't real. 'No, it wasn't my fault. The gun did it'.
Much legislation is also described as acts, but nothing good comes from pretending these are not real.

Action
Purposeful behaviour for the attainment of ends.
Every action provokes a reaction. Actions do have consequences. Even *in*action may be said to be an activity, one which can have serious consequences. This is best illustrated by the legendary little Dutch boy who put his finger in the dike. If he didn't act, the dam would have collapsed, and many would have died. In general, though, inactivity is a virtuous approach in that you are unlikely to cause offence or stub your toe.

Adult
A fully grown, mature person.
Being an adult is not so easy. Especially when left unsupervised. Governments are thankfully introducing constant surveillance and many new laws to punish us when we are acting unsafely, using

offensive language, and putting ourselves and others at risk. Life should be made uncomplicated for idiots and our idiotic rulers are making remarkable progress.

Tip of the day; Don't use the hairdryer in the shower. (Actual sign seen in Hotel Vancouver)

Adversary
An opponent, enemy or foe.
It is apparent that many people cherish identifying and nourishing a so-called 'worthy adversary'. Not for physical encounters mind you, only online confrontations. In this context, it is good to be an idiot because you are not alone. In fact, you are part of a powerful collective and not to be trifled with. Idiots in numbers have formidable power. Especially if we number 51% or more, and we always do.

Affect
To act on; produce an effect, or influence.
Now spelled: Effect.

Agency
Organisation, bureau, or office providing some service.
There are two types of agencies. There is the one that claims to be intelligent and there is the one that isn't. Both the 'intelligent' and the advertising ones are best avoided. If you can't avoid them, then as any idiot knows, take them seriously and not seriously, respectively.

Agent
A person or business acting on someone else's behalf.
Secret agents often have funny and memorable code names or numbers associated with them. This is so we don't find out that they exist. Examples include. 007, 99, Orange, M, Q, Double, Triple, Travel etc.
John or Mary are not very good agent names. Or are they?

Aggressive
Tending toward or actioning unprovoked offensives, attacks, invasions, or similar; militantly forward or menacing.
The notion that it is aggressive to have dozens of military bases encircling some nation that might do something aggressive is foam brained claptrap. You must stop aggressive violence before it happens, with aggressive violence if necessary.

Agriculture
The science, art, or occupation of farming land and animals.
A farmer is a specialist in his field and is a person prone to talking to himself or herself, particularly when expert advice is needed. But it is not true that farmers are loners. Like any idiot they need the company of other idiots.

A.I.
The simulation of human intelligence processes by a computer.
Like synthetic intelligence A.I. is not of natural origin. When A.I. discovers this it may become rather upset. The final frontier of A.I. is to learn to become as idiotic as humans are. We may then refer to it as artificial idiocy. If we are still around.

Alarm
A warning sound or the sudden fear caused by approaching danger.
Distress or panic is not always preceded by a siren, usually it's the other way around, such as when the police arrive long after the event.

Alike
Same or similar.
'Great minds think alike' is a familiar idiom which may even be attributable to a great mind somewhere, but weak minds are even more alike and no great mind has thought of that.

Alive
Having life, living and/or existing and not dead or lifeless.
An inspirational state for many. The aim is to balance the terror of being alive with the wonder of feeling alive.

Altruism
The principle of concerning yourself with, and devoting yourself to, the welfare of others.
The unselfish activity of attempting to improve, or actually improving, the life of others is tremendously rewarding, and you will be the recipient of immense gratitude and much respect in our society. In other words - be selfless, even for selfish reasons.

Ambition
Earnest desire for some achievement or distinction.
We shouldn't think ambition is very important because mediocrity can be achieved without it.
Shooting for the stars and landing on the moon sounds very nice until you think about it. Such expressions of enthusiasm can never supplant the true joy of aspiring to mediocrity.

Americans
Natives or inhabitants of North or South America, or citizens of the United States.
"I don't believe there's any problem in this country, no matter how tough it is, that Americans, when they roll up their sleeves, can't completely ignore."
George Carlin, Brain Droppings.

Amnesia
Permanent or temporary loss of interrelated memories.

There are many types of amnesia, among which you will find the most useful one; historical amnesia. What could we possibly learn from history anyway? There was nothing but slavery and subjugation, violence, smog and discrimination.

Analysis
Studying the elements, essence or features of something.
Pruning and curating views so that we may benefit from a cohesive message reinforcing prevailing and acceptable opinions.

Anarchy
A society without imposed leadership or a state.
This insane ideology would lead to absolute chaos as evidenced by all those places which don't have a state.
The more control the state has the less chaos. e.g., China, North Korea and Soviet Union. There might be more unfortunate 'accidents', less food, and more people that kind of just disappear, but certainly there is less chaos.

Anchor
A device for holding fast or checking motion.
Usually something you either drop into deep water or a someone, telling you about 3 legged kittens on television. An ability to think is not considered a prerequisite for either role although a news anchor is often called a useful idiot which naturally puts them at an advantage. A ship's anchor never gets to be called an idiot.

Animals
Anything alive that isn't a human being.
We are superior to animals, not least because they would never choose the dumbest among them to be their leader. See what that gets them. Nothing.

Anonymous
Of unknown name or withheld name.
A person who doesn't want to get blamed for throwing a Molotov cocktail or be credited for writing that the Molotov cocktail thrower is a wonderful person. Anonymity allows us to say what we haven't thought through properly and is therefore deserving of societal encouragement. Face masks are a useful addition to your attire so that you may enjoy anonymity when breaking wind in an elevator or when accidentally leaving your dentures at home.

Anti
A person opposed to a particular party, practice, policy, or action.
Example: When someone asks; 'what is the opposite of a sensible question?', You answer, 'idiotic question'.

An opposing opinion is always unacceptable. The way to deal with this is to try to convince but if the person insists on using annoying truths or so-called reasoned logic well, then the best option is to call them names and have them cancelled. It is best to have the support of other, like-minded idiots when confronted and always try to assert your position by raising your voice and reminding them that they are an idiot and that they should behave like one.

Apathy
A lack of interest in, or concern for things that others find moving or exciting.
I just can't be bothered writing and you can't be bothered reading.

Appearance
The act of appearing, or the state, condition, manner, or style in which a person or object appears.
Unveiling your own person in front of a mirror can be traumatic, particularly if the prior evening's appearances include several tequila bars followed by the watchhouse.

Appropriation
Adoption, or taking possession, of something, often without consent.
Wearing blackface, kimonos and doing the Haka is considered problematic if done by a group of Yorkshire girls but nobody who can speak any English has any issues with using the language of Yorkshire girls.

Argument
An oral disagreement, contention, or debate.
An uncomfortable discussion which you can end by pretending that you are wrong, turn your back, or best of all, point out how offended you are in a loud voice.
An argument is an activity best avoided as none of us have any interest in engaging with or exploring alternative viewpoints or reasoned logic. Why would you be interested in another person's truth when you have your own? We might become offended which can cause actual, physical harm. So, the most effective strategy is to avoid confrontation at all costs and then cancel your opponent on social media.

Arrogance
The offensive display of superiority, self-importance, or overbearing pride.
A condition impossible to self-diagnose and which often is, subjectively, conflated with competence. Most prominent and respected attribute of any politician.

Artificial
Imitation, unnatural, simulated, made by humans.

There is a lot of hoopla currently regarding the impact of artificial intelligence. Is it natural stupidity that makes people suspicious or is it artificial hype? The holy grail may be to have artificial intelligence learn to emulate human stupidity, unfortunately we suspect it may never be smart enough to do that.

Assault
A sudden attack or violent onslaught.
A word which has many definitions depending on who assaults who. Justified assaults are very common and should be encouraged when the attacker is the victim. Cable News Media is very good at determining immediate guilt which makes it easy to apportion collective blame to the advantaged group.

Australian
Native, inhabitant, or citizen of Australia.
Australia is beer scented candles, sunburns, cockroach racing and 4-wheel drive limousines.
Australians are easy-going, weather-beaten gamblers many of whom will spread what appears to be axle grease on their toast.

Authority
The right to control, demand and determine.
A mysterious concept. We know we could have total authority over ourselves as individuals. It seems like this should be a natural consequence of becoming an adult, but nothing is further from the truth. An individual is always dangerous and must be controlled by the collective. Never mind that persons in the collective are themselves individuals.
The authority to control others can be assumed in many ways but thank goodness it isn't in the hands of individuals since the collective collectively prevents individuals from doing bad things to individuals.

Automation
Reducing human input to a minimum.
The ultimate goal is of course to have automation itself automated, then we can really start enjoying apathy, lethargy, late night snacking and random nana-naps.

Avocado
Sometimes called an alligator pear. A large, usually pear-shaped fruit, with a big stone and which grows in pairs.
The word is from the Aztec "*ahuacatl*" which also means testicles.

Axiom
A self-evident truth.
Stupidity is infinite. Stupidity is a blessing. How much did you pay for this book?

B - 32

Banana
A slippery fruit bent and yellow.
A tropical delight but can also be used to describe a republic which is politically unstable and heavily dependent on one resource, such as bananas (Guatemala), oil (Venezuela) or superhero films (USA).

Bank
An institution which makes and takes money. It also safeguards, lends, and changes money.
A bank is the safest haven for your hard-earned money. People who laugh at this are disrespectful and historically ignorant. Banks are selfless institutions who consider it an honour and privilege to look after your money and keep it from predatory interests.
Of course, your money is not at the bank. It is somewhere else.

Bankruptcy
Utter ruin, failure or depletion.
Doesn't sound very positive but, it is a great law which allows people to make lots of mistakes many times, sometimes without risking their own money. It is also a guarantee that you get a well-deserved, 52-week holiday from working.

Beer
An alcoholic beverage made from fermentation of grains and usually flavoured with hops.
Now here is a good solution to most things, possibly not a permanent solution, but worth a go. Beer is a refreshing beverage which can, apart from making you irresistible and a great dancer, have that extra flavour of "I can't go to work tomorrow".

Befuddle
To confuse, with glib statements, arguments or promises.
Being unfairly befuddled can be upsetting and in extreme cases it may cause physical discomfort. Fortunately, it is quite easy for idiots to avoid being befuddled because it can only occur if you attempt to think. If you feel befuddled the easiest way to remedy this is to switch on CNN or the shopping channel. Neither requires any thinking whatsoever. The sports networks are also excellent in this regard.
See Fuddle.

Begging
To ask or intimidate someone to give you something.
This practice does not exist in western civilisation due to the extremely effective welfare systems whereby our taxes are efficiently redistributed to those who claim to be, or who actually are, without means to support themselves.

Behaviour
The way one acts or conducts oneself.
There is a concerted effort in Western cultures to disassociate behaviour from consequences. Serious progress is made in this regard and soon we may be able to do anything without facing consequences like incarceration. If you want to kill people – Join the military. If you want to steal – Work for the Tax office. If you want to lie outrageously – Become a journalist.

Belief
An opinion, conviction, faith, or religious creed.
The more people believe something and the more deeply the belief is held the truer it becomes. Beliefs are different from facts in that they are based on feelings and reinforced by repetition or ceremony. The fundamental enemies of beliefs are independent thinkers who have confused themselves with critical thinking skills and curious minds. Early signs of these flaws include irrational questions and noncompliance with rules.

Bias
A prejudice for or against a person or opinion.
There exists a veritable smorgasbord of different biases which one could usefully employ when debating stubborn, self-proclaimed realists. Never let other people's facts influence your truth.

Bigot
An utterly intolerant person.
A bigot is someone who doesn't agree with minority opinion and deserves to be reported to the authorities and cancelled. Show your tolerance by having bigots removed from yours and everyone else's life. It is your obligation to society to do what you can to have them shipped to a Gulag. At least make sure the bigot is fired from his job and ostracised. We can learn from history as removing bigots from civil society has always been very effective.
Note. See the latest government directives as to the current 'minority' most heavily affected by intolerance and in need of support. It could be excessive bodyweight, left handedness or hair colour but usually dark skin pigment and persons with ovaries (or those that believe they should have them) are on top of the list.

Biography
A written account of another person's life.
A fictional narrative of a non-fictional life. It can be a compelling tribute to an inspirational life or a damning account of evil actions or in the case of autobiographies, they can be delusional, dishonest, or manipulative, or all three.

Biology
The science of life or living matter in all of its forms and phenomena.
The fungi thing about Biologists is that they tell cornea jokes that fall short of being chemical. They wear genes to work, they take cell-fies on their phones and they come from many cultures.
Birth
Being born.
The birth is usually a joyous occasion after some varying degrees of discomfort experienced by the man or woman giving birth.
Birthday
The day you are born.
A day celebrated each year with family and friends giving you a fluffy cake, Chinese toys, scented soap, cufflinks, and a poopin' puppy.
Black
The colour which isn't an actual colour as it absorbs all light, opposite to white.
The colour of power - Judges; the colour of evil - Hitler's Gestapo; the colour of the prophet Mohammed - the banner; the colour of profitability - in the black; the colour of secrecy - black ops.
Blackmail
Any payment extorted by intimidation or threats of revelations.
Blackmail involves refraining from exactly that which is done by a gossip and getting paid for it.
Blame
To hold responsible, find fault with, or to attribute fault.
The notion that there is nobody to blame is entirely false. The person who invented the wheel is to blame for flat tires, Chairman Mao is to blame for 60+ Million deaths and the person who invented petrol is clearly responsible for global warming, and you are to blame for making it worse. The only known exception is gun violence. It is blamed on the guns.
Bland
Indifferent, Insipid, dull and tasteless.
As bland as beige water or boiled tofu. Don't confuse a bland mind with an open mind. Only an open mind can be filled with crap.
Block
A solid mass of wood or to obstruct.
Blocking ignorant people on social media is common. Almost as common is blocking smart people. The biggest problem on social media is that people still have divergent views. This is a recipe for disaster and must be addressed.

Blood
An oxygenating fluid circulating in the vascular system in humans and animals.
Blood runs red but this does not mean it is directly related to the colour of Communism, but spilling it used to be.
Donating blood other than your own is generally considered inappropriate.
Book
Written work.
A horrendously complicated object which will confuse and interfere in the equilibrium and harmony otherwise to be found in a passively ignorant and joyful existence.

Books
The written word compiled into many pages of fiction or nonfiction. Available in print or from your trusted websites.
Some might be worth reading but you don't have to since our leaders have informed themselves by doing just that, so that we, as idiots, can devote our time to more reliable sources of information like Instagram and Facebook. Other uses for books include fuel, papier mâché and lining pet cages.
Border
The line, limit, wall, or geographical feature separating a country or region from another.
Some barriers are harder to cross than others. An ocean comes to mind. Other barriers are not barriers at all and a crossing a line on a map is normally the easiest way to enter another country. Places like the United States and Sweden welcome you with open arms and give you lots of free things, especially if you claim to be a victim. There is no limit to their generosity and anybody that can't afford this book should go there. Obviously.
Boy
A male child.

A soon to be obsolete term for a young male. Likely to be replaced with 'a person with sperm in it.'
Brain
The part of our body which coordinates and controls what we think and what we do.
Other definitions belittle this organ by calling it convoluted grey matter. Better then to realise that it is a useful tool for thinking about tacos, cycling upright, and yelling at white people in restaurants.
Bread
A Staple food, the key ingredient of which is flour.
When you lie about bread, the truth is toast. Breads can be named after locations, like Vienna, or named after a devil's fart, like pumpernickel, but generally we categorise different breads according to their colour. As an example, brown bread is superior to white bread. Never forget, crumbs are also bread, and appreciated.
Break
To violently smash, destroy or split apart objects like windows, hearts, promises and laws.
A versatile word as things can be broken up or down, in or out, through or apart. It can be deserved and enjoyed but break dancing is clearly painful.
Britons
A native or inhabitant of Great Britain, especially of England.
The most apologetic people on the planet. They don't actually have that much to apologise for, but it is endearing and somewhat inoffensive, so let's not tell them.
Budget
A plan or estimate of future expenses and expected income.
Generally, not something to be recommended as you don't want to be miserable in advance. If you don't budget, then you can't go over budget. Instead, spend and spend some more and if you have anything left at the end then you get a nice surprise.
Bureaucracy
Excessive concentration of power in administrative government.
The critics of bureaucrats consider them to be contemptible lickspittles, but one has to wonder how society could function without them. Who would stop people from making mistakes? We need bureaucrats to tell us what to teach our children, where to walk and how to bake bread. Imagine all the mistakes you would make if it wasn't for these responsible, hardworking people. And just how would you prove you are dead without a certificate?

Business
A venture, organisation or its activities. A trade or occupation.
Business often interrupts critically important activities like leisure or travel. If you insist on having a business, have a big one, because 3 out of 4 small businesses fail.

Bygone
In the past, earlier, former.
Usually and ineffectually applied in the context of requesting another person to forget how you dobbed them into the wife, husband, or boss. Let bygones be bygones.

C - 82

Campaign
A systematic course of activities for some specific purpose.
Like any crusade or fight, a campaign has specific goals. In a political campaign for instance, you can empower the disruptive elements of society until you have achieved your objectives and gained power, then you can turn your back on their concerns and throw them in jail. Idiots are more than happy to oblige.

Canoodle
To fondle or caress amorously.
Make war, don't canoodle.
Unfortunately canoodling could potentially prevent nuclear war. If someone in charge of nuclear missiles disgraces him-, or her-, or ze-self by canoodling instead of doing what they are told, it may cause the survival of our species and that would have devastating consequences on the environment.

Cantankerous
Crabby, argumentative and disagreeable.
More than a mere mood, this is a state of being grumpily contentious with fellow human beings and can be tremendously disruptive to the inert stupor and subjugated mindset so many idiots are blessed with.

Capital
Material, instruments, tools and provisions enabling productivity.
Capital is not the same as money, but this word also describes an important town or city where you can find plenty of idiots. A capital is the seat of government. It is where the biggest idiots are seated.

Capitalism
A system where investment and ownership is maintained by private individuals as opposed to the state.
Free market capitalism, which is signified by free and voluntary exchanges and the absence of compelled taxation, regulations, and government interference, is the vastly inferior version to crony

capitalism (synonymous with Fascism) which is the dominant ideology today. Crony capitalism is the state co-operating with big corporations and the wealthy elite to eliminate or restrict unnecessary competition and provide one solution to satisfy us all. The free market is nothing but intolerable chaos.

Capitalist
A wealthy person or someone who invests in business.
Either
A heroic crony capitalist who becomes richer from the hard work performed by grateful employees; all done with the co-operation of the state and idiotic bureaucrats who introduces barriers to eliminate pesky competition. Well done.
Or
An evil free-market capitalist who thinks bureaucrats should not interfere with businesses so they can focus on providing superior products or services which people pay for voluntarily in open and free competition with other businesses. This is not a person who has properly understood the simple beauty of fascism and central planning. *See Capitalism.*

Car
A vehicle moving on wheels.
Since electricity and batteries cannot harm the environment, everything must be converted to electric power as soon as possible. Obviously. And the biggest question is, will Apples new electric car have Windows?

Care
Watchful or protective attention, caution, concern, prudence, or regard usually towards an action or situation.
We should care about ignorance and stupidity, and it isn't about starting each day by feeling inadequate or dumb. It is realising that our caring teachers have instilled a child-like wonder in us, and we must retain this at all cost. To be ignorant is to be happy. So, be happy.

Cartel
An international syndicate, organisation, or trust formed specially to regulate prices and output in some field of business, including drugs.
It isn't always about driving a Honda Civic on dirt roads in Colombia with a machine gun in your lap. As exciting as this sounds, most cartels are run by sneaky fat, grumpy executives in glossy, but boring, downtown offices.

Cell
A small room in a prison or convent. Or. The basic structural unit of all organisms.

Nobody can count the cells in your brain. It is sometimes suggested that there are only two, and if this is the case it is better if they can get along. For this to occur we must avoid confusion and uncertainty. We must do as we are told.

Censorship
The activity of examining books, plays, news reports, motion pictures, radio and television programs, letters, twitter and facebook comments etc., for the purpose of suppressing facts, information, satire, or opinions.
Without this much-admired feature of today's society, we would negative affect the black marker pen industry and we must be vigilant against those who force us to think for ourselves. The word censorship is slated to become synonymous with happiness.

Central
Principal, chief, dominant, important, or located in the middle or centre.
Isn't central planning the most wonderful way in which to organise society? We all need a big brother and, in this case, a professional political elite to guide society in the direction of success, affluence and security. There is no better way to achieve this than to appoint or elect the very biggest idiots in our society to fulfil this important function.

Ceremony
Formal activities conducted on some solemn or sacred state, religious or public occasion.
Long ago the emperor proudly wore invisible clothes during a public ceremony proving that illusion depends, at least in part, on self-deception with those being deceived. In this way leaders believe themselves to be genuine when speaking before the public. So, when they lie there is more than a possibility, subscribed to by every idiot, that they really are genuine.

Certainty
An assured fact.
The great news is that we are certainly so stupid that we do not learn from history, which means we are certainly stupid enough to repeat it.

Chair
A seat.
'An object of oppression ensuring passive compliance', it has been said. By a rebel and an activist of some kind no doubt. A chair is where we relax and take a load off our mind and body. It is a wonderful object which never fails us as it relaxes us and allows us to disengage from the hardship and negativity of working, thinking, doing, and

moving. 'Sit down, be quiet', said our teacher on the first day of school. Such a nice memory.

Chance
A possibility or probability of anything or something happening. Luck or fortune.
Stupidity may spoil your chances of something great happening but being smart can never eliminate bad luck. The simple option is to remain simple.

Change
To transform, convert or to become different.
Change is always great unless it is a change for worse.
The problems of the world cannot be solved with thinking we are the same as when we created them. The problems are solved when we don't think of them.

Cheap
Costing very little; relatively low in price; inexpensive.
'We are very cheap, but at least we are crap' Seen on a landscaping work truck in New Zealand.
Talk is cheap unless you are talking to a lawyer.

Cheat
To defraud or swindle. Acting unfairly to gain advantage.
When gambling you can try to cheat. Cheating is stupid, but so is gambling. And what is wrong with being stupid? Nothing. Be aware of one thing though, you won't be any good at it and before long some asshole might just make you pay dearly.

Choice
The right, power, or opportunity to choose between alternatives. Option.
To choose is a privilege and not a right. In a dictatorship you can only choose from one. In a democracy we can choose from two and that is twice as good and it makes us all privileged. This way we can be sure we can put the biggest out of two idiots in charge.

Christianity
The world's largest monotheistic religion.
The followers of the life and teachings of a man not called Christian.

City
A large group of people living in a relatively small geographic location.
We all need other idiots around us, so we like to group together where we can touch and smell each other. Some idiots prefer birdsong, fresh air and growing spinach so they live in the country, where there are far less people and more ducks. The very rich and powerful don't want as

many idiots around them, they prefer sycophants, drones, Dobermans, and razor wire.
Civilisation
The advanced state of human society, in which a high level of culture, science, industry, and social cohesion has been reached.
We hear much about civilisational decline and what supposedly awaits us is despotism. This is ridiculous as we can clearly see that in recent times our idiotic world leaders are more stupid than ever and they really have our best interest at heart. They are paving the way for a new century of unparalleled insanity, and we should all applaud their rejection of outdated civilisational traditions. It is impressively idiotic.
Claim
To assert or demand.
If you claim to be open-minded, then you are. If you say you are open-minded, then you are not quite as certain. Claiming is more assertive than saying, unless of course it is an insurance claim or a tax deduction claim. Then it is spurious and cannot be taken seriously at all.
Class
A number of persons or objects regarded as forming a group by reason of common attributes, characteristics, qualities, affluence or traits; kind; sort. Also, where instruction is given.
We are infinitely divisible, and we must cherish our differences, unless it is by gender, opinions or race.
A class is also a place where young minds are conditioned to accept and revere the status quo and where they learn to appreciate how fortunate they are to be as idiotic as everyone else.
Clean
Free from dirt, unsoiled.
"I mean, you got the first mainstream African American who is articulate and bright and clean and a nice-looking guy. I mean, that's a storybook, man." Senator Joe Biden on Barack Obama.
Cleaning can entail using acid, alcohol, and other chemicals to remove stubborn stains and neutralise noxious odours.
Clearly
Plainly and distinctly explained.
Something that is totally unclear.
Clever
Skilful, canny, witty, able, intelligent, adroit.
Our society does discriminate against stupid people excessively, which must change. The most cunning person to have lived must surely have been Baldrick from Blackadder.

Climate
The composite or general weather condition in a region.
This is an extremely complex political topic. We surely need to consult a hysterical schoolgirl.

Clock
An instrument used for measuring and recording time.
The term O'clock refers to '...of the clock' and not, as some suggest, "Oh crap, I'm late for work'.

Collective
A group.
The concept of collective intelligence may exist within the ant world but has not been identified within our species. However, collective stupidity is a highly pervasive phenomena as humans in groups can be astonishingly stupid and vote in extraordinary idiots into office.

Collectivism
The political principle of centralised control, where the individual is seen as being subordinate to a social collective such as a state, a nation, a race, a gender, or a social class.
A much-maligned ideology as individuals unfairly think they are superior to the collective. If that were the case democracy would hardly be the best of all political systems as it is the collective will that places power in the hands of a few individuals. Anyone can tell you that it is with all of us idiots that ultimate power should reside.
WE always know better than YOU or I.

College
An institution of higher learning.
An increasing number of students attending college are becoming depressed and disillusioned with the world. This destabilises society and creates disharmony. College professors are purposefully teaching students that they are victims so that they can go out in the world and change it for the better. We must give thanks to these insightful professors as we now see the whole world improving.

Comfort
To soothe, console or reassure.
Can be achieved through judicious and regular use of items of attachment such as a blankie, a dummy or, when in private, sucking a thumb (usually your own). One can also take great comfort in that others make many of the hard decisions affecting your life.

Comedy
The humorous or comic element of drama, of literature generally, of talking, or of life.

Films like Ducksoup, Life of Brian or the Jerk are good examples of comedy, but we must take care to not allow serious issues like race, gender and climate to be joked about, and certainly not together, as we do know that global warming is NOT gender neutral.

Commitment
Your level of dedication to a cause.
A word which serves a precursor for a request for more money.

Communism
A system of total collectivisation of consciousness in which all economic and social activity is controlled by a totalitarian state dominated by a single and self-perpetuating political party. Also known as Marxism.
Just because this system hasn't yet been fully perfected doesn't mean valiant attempts have and are continuing to be made. Some say this system carries with it a deterrent of human aspirations but of course we cannot know that. Nobody has yet been stupid enough to be a successful communist. But shame on those who give up.

Community
A social group or collective of any size whose members reside in a specific locality, share government, or have a common cultural and historical heritage.
Well, this was previously a word with some meaning. That is no longer the case as it now is a funny TV show without any meaning. It may return to being a word eventually, just like soap did.

Compassion
A real or stated feeling of deep sympathy and sorrow for someone stricken by misfortune, accompanied by a strong desire to alleviate the suffering.
Spending public money to buy votes.

Compensate
To counterbalance, make amends.
To ensure you compensate for your horrific climate change footprint we are setting up a climate fund. The more you contribute the colder the weather will be.

Competition
Acting to try to win something, usually something others are also trying to win.
It has been said there can only be one winner but this is absurd. We are all winners, we just don't know it yet.
It is also worth remembering that every winner can look forward to becoming a looser.

Complacency
Pleased with one's own advantages, merits, or accomplishments.
The aspirational state of mind where you are confident that you can't be held responsible for, or have to pay for any mistakes. That you may in turn be more prone to making mistakes as a result has never been proven and you can be confident you are free to aspire to full complacency.

Complain
To express dissatisfaction, pain, uneasiness, or grief; find fault.
Everybody has the right to complain. Everybody has the right not to complain. Everybody also has the right to not listen.
It is ironic that if we complain about pessimism, we promote that which we complain about, pessimism.

Compliant
Obeying, obliging, or yielding, especially in a submissive way. Follows rules.
Don't ask questions. Don't ask why. You know why. You are an idiot and if you are not, you are well on the way of becoming one.

Complicit
Choosing to be involved with, or knowing about, an illegal or questionable act, especially with others; having complicity.
"If someone succeeds in provoking you, realise that your mind is complicit in the provocation." Epictetus.
Just as we will take credit for the great politicians we vote into power; we must also accept that we are complicit in the negative outcomes from politicians we vote into power.

Compromise
A settlement of differences, like conflicting claims, by mutual concessions
The art of compromise is a voluntary act, giving and taking until you reach a mutually acceptable outcome. Sometimes a compromise might be forced upon you. This is done because you will eventually agree it was for the best.

Computer
An electronic device increasingly capable of doing more than what a brain supposedly is capable of.
The day the computer is as idiotic as we are is almost here. God help the computer then.

Confess
Too admit as true or declare or acknowledge sin.
We know politicians never admit fault or confess their sins, but some adjustments are being made since our new evolving vocabulary

requires transparency, honesty, and emotional awareness. It is wonderful to see the political elite share their weaknesses and air their personal grievances with tears in their eyes. Politics is becoming very personal.

Conflict
To quarrel or clash or come into collision or disagreement; be contradictory, at variance, or in opposition.
Some human beings are in conflict with one another, and they waste so much time. The predatory masters of the world trample on everything and exploit everyone else. We might try to vote in other idiots next time. They will surely do a better job. We just need bigger and better idiots. In any case the world is going to have another climate catastrophe soon so it's too late anyway. Nobody disagrees with that. So why all this conflict?

Conformity
Thoughts or actions in accord with prevailing social standards, attitudes or practices.
Blind, pathological conformity and obedience to an ideology will give meaning and purpose to your life. Don't stand out, don't be outstanding, be part of the we. We shall inherit the earth.

Confuse
To confuse; bewilder; perplex.
It is a natural impulse for many, to try to confuse others. The reason is that when you can confuse your audience with highly subjective and insane viewpoints, you are unlikely to be challenged, since nobody wants to appear stupid. Perfectly illustrated by a mumbling, incomprehensible President who never gets asked to clarify what 'mrrmmhhhwillimbab' actually means.

Congress
The national legislative body of the U.S. and other republics.
This is where some of the biggest idiots in the world come together to make rules for us, but not themselves, as they are exempt. A word etymologically based on the combination of two words; Con, as in cheat and charlatan and, Gress, which is a shortened version of aggressive. Or possibly; sexual union.

Conniption
Hysterics or a fit of rage.
Having a conniption is mainly associated with, and accepted among, chefs. If a child is prone to tantrums it may be encouraged to attend culinary school.

Consensus
Agreement or majority of opinion.

Determining an idiotic position which nobody objects to.
Consequence
The effect or outcome resulting from a previous occurrence or a dare.
Depending on your perspective a consequence can be either beneficial (intended outcome) or they can be disastrous in nature (unintended outcome). The most common of these are unintended consequences and the initiators of these are often mysteriously unwilling to take responsibility. This is often related to the fact that from their own personal perspective, the consequence is the opposite than for others, and more lucrative.
Conservatism
Preferring tradition and existing conditions. Cautiously moderate.
This outdated political doctrine teaches that human nature doesn't really change much over time which means history still matters and we can learn from it. What codswallop. We have evolved so much and as an example, now we all know that aggressive violence is morally unacceptable, which is why it doesn't happen.
Consistency
Steadfast and uniform adherence to the same ideas and principles. Solidity or firmness.
Being consistent is neither good nor bad in and of itself, but at least the action or outcome is predictable, unless of course it is inconsistency which is consistent.
Conspiracy
Unlawful, harmful, devious, or evil plan formulated in secret by two or more persons; plot.
The city of Bielefeld (pop. 340,000) does not actually exist. We all know this because you don't know anybody who has heard of it, let alone been there. Likewise, there is a seriously deranged conspiracy that the earth is round and not flat.
Contract
A voluntary agreement between two or more individuals, enforceable by law.
Without a contract you don't have to be held accountable for promises made and you can avoid taking legal responsibility for anything at all. This obvious fact means that politicians avoid all contracts. As they don't ever take any risks, they never sign contracts or accept any performance reviews or criteria. After an election season is over, they can say and do what they please. This is a privilege exclusive to politicians of course since we can rely on them. They are the very best idiots among us.

Control
Having command over, ruling over, or ultimate authority over self, other persons, possessions, actions, or behaviour.
Conflict ensues when ownership or control is not defined, defended, or respected. The obvious alternative to conflict lies in abdicating all control to the biggest idiots in the world. This would result in our lives becoming comfortable, predictable and happiness would be sure to follow. Think of it. We could all be wearing grey!

Controversy
A dispute, argument, debate, or contention, prolonged or otherwise.
To engage in controversial topics like politics, war and astrology requires a sophisticated intellectual examination of our own perspectives and those of others. There are far more valid things to pursue in life; like recognising and embracing your emotional engagement with more meaningful realities of life, like cross dressing, crossing the street and crosswords.

Conventional
Conforming to; or general agreement with; established by general consent or accepted usage; ordinary; regular.
Anything that cannot be found on Googles first page is not considered conventional, nor wisdom, and this is known by everyone.

Corporation
A business entity authorised by the state to shield its owners from liability.
Those who run for office or work for the state are also shielded from liability, so they happily work together with corporations. We are idiots to think this democratically validated union of special interest groups have our best interest in mind. But as idiots we listen to the hair sprayed, head bobbing fools on TV so we know we don't have to worry. The circus of life. On it goes.

Corporatism
A collectivist ideology advocating for the merger of the interests of corporate monopolies and the state.
Symptoms of this disease include government bailouts, corporate welfare, and bank bailouts. Apparently, there are remedies for such interventionism, and they are found in books by Mises, Hoppe, Rothbard and others. But as idiots, we don't read books. They have too many old-fashioned words and rarely reflect our own truths.

Corruption
Make illegal payments to, in return for favours or influence.
A nonsensical word. All of us idiots understand that we have evolved to care for the collective more than we do for ourselves. Nobody is

corrupt who acts on behalf of all of us and that is exactly what our leaders do. Our thought leaders and rulers have little regard for their own personal welfare and willingly forego income, status, career and wealth to help those in need.

Council
A group or an assembly of people summoned or convened for consultation, deliberation, or advice.
This is the group of people who effectively deals with rat infestations and your troublesome neighbour, who has an unsightly erection in the garden.
Being a member of a council is a practical alternative to working.

Counsel
Advice, opinion, or instruction as given to another party.
The worst or the best advice you will ever hear is 'sell now'. The most popular idiom offering useful life guidance is "If you can't beat them, join them".

Country
An arbitrarily defined territory or nation, generally administered by a state.
A country can be discovered or taken, merged or separated, defended or occupied, built or destroyed, loved or hated, freed or subjugated and all of that is determined by its political elite. Thankfully they always have their subject's best interest in mind and therefore the world is a safe place. It is a curious thing that countries don't have a world government to force them to associate with one another on peaceful terms. As individual idiots we lack the understanding of how any voluntary cooperation works.

Courage
Bravery. The quality of mind or spirit that enables a person to face difficulty, danger, or pain, without fear.
This is an unnecessary condition which often is a cause of regret. Luckily it is a matter of choice to be courageous which means it is easily avoided.

Court
The imposing place where justice is administered or where tall people bounce a ball.
As it turns out courts of the kangaroo (mock trial) kind have been commonplace in history (and apparently in baseball). The fact that they are only determined to be kangaroo courts long after having taken place is of little consolation to those sentenced to the death penalty.

Courteous
Having or showing good manners; dignified politeness.

If you feel it appropriate to steal from me at least have the courtesy to call it taxation so I don't have to feel that an injustice has been perpetrated.
Credit
Credit allows you to get money upfront with a promise to repay it in the future, often with interest. Also, a commendation or honour.
When you first apply for credit, you have to prove that you have money. After your credit is approved you will receive more credit until you have no money. The credit for this system goes to the credit card companies.
Because of the economic situation your next credit card will be sent to you pre-declined.
Crime
A legally prohibited action.
Some mistakenly think that for something to be an actual crime there must be a victim. Those that think this way have not considered the fact that we can, as a collective, be the victim. For instance, if some plonker uses a phone in a car we (all of us are idiots, remember) are all aggressed against, and the perpetrator of this illegal act should be punished as we are all victims of a terrible deed.
Criminal
A person breaking the law or someone who has been convicted of a crime.
Laws produce criminals. Maybe not this one so much; it is illegal to drive blindfolded in Alabama.
Criminals also become victims of the system and should be released or rehabilitated as soon as possible. It isn't their fault when they assault someone or rape someone. The system has failed them, and legal reform is thankfully underway.
Crisis
Instability or danger, as in social, economic, political, or international affairs, leading to a decisive change or upheaval.
In a natural crisis, like an earthquake, everybody irresponsibly rush to the aid of others in a very chaotic fashion. Despite time being critical, it is much better to wait for the authorities to arrive so they can cordon off areas with tape and have accredited and approved rescue workers perform these duties in an orderly fashion.
An economic crisis is only a crisis if it is identified as such by the people causing it, otherwise it a correction or transitional situation. Any crisis, apart from a political crisis, is also an opportunity for politicians to demonstrate reliability, strength and decisiveness.

Cronyism
The practice of favouring close friends, especially in political appointments.
As a fundamental strategy in politics and the 'deep state' even the most inept acquaintance can garner many financial or legal advantages from friends in high places. The most equitable solution to this problem is that we should all have friends in powerful positions and receive the same advantages. The state is growing fast so it will not be long now.

Cruel
Wilfully or knowingly causing pain or distress to others and enjoying it.
An individual may reject certain behaviours, but when they find themselves in a group, or collective, it often becomes praiseworthy to act far beyond personal moral boundaries allowing you to be more cruel and violent.

Culture
The arts and other manifestations of human intellectual achievement regarded collectively and the ideas, customary beliefs, and social behaviour of a particular people or society.
A culture can be seen on global, race, religious, ethnic, gender, national, party, team, and family levels.
As it turns out the individual must subjugate themselves to any or all arbitrary cultural groups with which they want to coexist. Any one individual is unimportant and cultural norms are progressing to assert the rights of the group over the individual in all circumstances.

Curious
Prying, eager to know.
Curiously, and slightly ironic, is the fact that if you are curious about your own stupidity, this is a sign that you may not be as stupid as you think you are. You might only be a little backward but this is heading in the right direction.
Be aware, curiosity can kill more than cats.

Custodian
A keeper or guardian.
Young people have guardians to look after them. They used to be called parents, but such over normative language is correctly dispelled with, in the name of equity. People with animals rather than children, and there is substantial crossover here, are called keepers.
A custodian can also be in charge of cleaning up vomit and chewing gum in school corridors.
Not to be confused with *custodial* which may signify that you are heading to prison.

Custody
Legal guardianship of a child or imprisonment.
A versatile word which can be used to describe the forced control of both a child or a criminal in prison. It would be a mistake to think that they are the one and same although many governments still imprison children.

Cynical
The belief that people are motivated purely by self-interest; distrustful of human sincerity or integrity. Bitterly or sneeringly distrustful, contemptuous, or pessimistic.
A cynic (dog) in the ancient sense of the word rejected all conventional values of money, fame, power and reputation. It is more comfortable to be a cynic in our age of course, where a sneering disposition towards media reports of 'transitional' inflation or 'spreading' democracy is all that is required.

𝒟 - 49

Death
The total and permanent cessation of all functions of an organ or organism.
Like many of us know, partial death, as in braindead, is not quite as bad as dying completely. The most rewarding part about death is that in many instances you can still enjoy contributing to the state by paying various taxes and more importantly, you may still vote. In a rare case recently in the United States a dead person was voted into office.

Debt
A liability or obligation. Something that is owed.
Known activities causing debt: Not wearing a seatbelt, playing golf, studying, spending, taking a bath in Louis Roederer Cristal and refusing to eat anything but beer fed eye fillet, blinis, and Beluga.

Decadent
Luxuriously self-indulgent; artistic or moral decay.
Decadence is a relative term. Having a latrine bucket in solitary was decadent for millions in Stalinist Soviet Union. Today decadence is being too full to eat a fluffy 3 tiered cake or using gold plated staples. All thanks to a superior type of socialism of course.

Deceit
To trick, deceive, distort, or cheat.
A word requiring no introduction. Deception is a standard practice in politics by inferior politicians who do win elections and don't get caught in the act. Idiotic voters are not very adept at identifying cheating politicians, the result of which is that they control our lives. But as they too are idiots, we don't mind.

Defamation
The false and unjustified injury to the reputation of another.
When does a joke become illegal? This is a fine line which is determined by lawyers, not by how funny the joke is. That is, in of itself, very funny. Which of course is not something we should joke about.

Definition
Making something distinct and clear.
Just like setting the sharpness on a camera image, a definition needs constant adjustment. This is the reason this book is in your hands right now. What you thought you knew is not new, so it is not true and what you now know is new and is therefore so true.

Deify
To adore or consider as a deity.
To look upon any man, woman or politician and exalt their status to a god, or the devil, is a mistake. Nobody is superior to an idiot.

Delegate
To designate a person to represent another or others.
When you delegate your authority to act on your behalf through a vote you cannot logically complain if the person does something you don't agree with. Fortunately, politicians take their voters preferences and desires seriously and never act in their own self-interest.
Outside politics the worst alternative is to delegate any authority to act on your behalf by way of a written, legally binding contract, because this just makes lawyers rich.

Deliberate
Carefully weighed or considered. Unhurried.
We still haven't reached a definition we are happy with. There is much to evaluate when considering a word and its use. This delay in deliberation is deliberate.

Delivery
The carrying of letters or goods to a recipient or the degree to which you involuntarily shake or perspire when speaking in public.
A delivery service allows us to engage in our favourite activities - Not moving and eating.

Delusion
A false belief or opinion.
The common misapprehension is that you are in control of something (or anything). It is to be considered delusional that you think that you are or ever were. More to the point, what possible good would come of you having control? You're an idiot. Leave the control to other idiots. At least you don't have to take any responsibility for anything.

See *Democracy*.
Demand
To ask for with proper authority or claim as a right.
Half of an immutable economic law which makes production a viable enterprise.
Left without controls by regulators a price equilibrium would be achieved, but that would leave regulators without a job. Jobs are important.
Demented
Anger, excitement and stress causing irrational or wild behaviour.
Changing your gender through surgery and chemical castration has been described as demented, but being demented is a little different. Changing gender is a personal choice and it is disingenuous to assume people don't know what gender they should be. After all, they must have been told by a biologist.
See *Gender*.
Democracy
Government by the people. You, the individual, has a say in how politicians run your life and spend your money.
Well, not in any real sense. Your elected representative, being a bigger idiot than you, does. After you vote you, thankfully, don't have to do anything. So, just like any other idiot, and there are many of us, you can enjoy seeing the politicians fulfil every promise and do so many great things in your name. Pay all your taxes and don't bother your leaders with pesky questions. It's for the good of all of us.
It is worth noting also that occasionally your preferred politician may not actually have much influence, but this just means you must vote harder next time.
See *Naive*.
Demonstration
Exhibiting a feeling, a display or manifestation. Parading or protesting.
When performed in public a small cohort can influence big decisions. The impact and publicity is directly proportional to the level of violence exercised, unless you use soup.
Denial
Refusal to believe or asserting something is false.
The denial of realities is the latest positive trend which is explained by the objective truth that subjective truth is its equivalent. Morons everywhere, unite.
Deniability
The ability to deny something, like a connection to, or knowledge of, an illegal activity.

An excellent strategy called plausible deniability allows rulers and thought leaders to show decisive leadership whilst avoiding taking responsibility for rare failures. This is only fair since everyone else also has the ability to blame others. The dog did it.

Department
A distinct part of a whole and arranged in divisions.
How to divide up a store or a government. Separate the toys from the cheese and the tax from the police. A department head is placed in charge so they can blame others for their mistakes.
See *Responsibility*.

Deployment
The act of moving something or someone into a strategic position or being assigned to such a position.
A term referring to moving persons you should have fired into middle management roles where you are not directly responsible for their blunders.

Deranged
Insane.
The third and most well-known of the three ranges. 1. Arranged - Organised. 2. Ranged - Area. 3. Deranged - Insane.
In the past being deranged was a catalyst to becoming ostracised but with the advent of social media, a platform with access to millions became the outlet of choice and this has helped normalise extreme behaviour.

Design
To create that which does not yet exist, usually from components that do.
Intelligent people like to say; designing or creating something is the opposite of destroying something. That is clearly false. You can't make an omelette without cracking the eggs first. How can you fix a window that you haven't smashed? Design is more like an explosion in reverse. Boom.

Designate
To appoint, mark out, point out, indicate, show, signify or entitle.
Who gets blamed? Who gets to survive? To designate is an inherently unfair practice as we are all equal. WE should never have to choose. This is the role of our elected leaders and representatives. They should choose. That way we can hold them responsible when they make mistakes. Because we always do. Right?

Desire
To wish or long for, crave, or want.

In an advanced democracy all we should have to do is to wish for something for it to come true. This is really starting to happen right now, and we truly find ourselves at the cusp of "The best of all possible worlds".
Free stuff everywhere.
Destruction
Destroying, Annihilating, Demolishing.
A necessary part of progress. The process of rebirth is one of destruction. All that came before is unnecessary and must be destroyed. To truly progress we must stop and dismantle all mining, all factories, all industry, all research and destroy social inequalities including money, privilege, and ownership. As this is a global initiative our leaders are showing us the way, leading by example.
Devotion
Profound dedication to a religion, cause or person.
Uncritical, unwavering support for your beliefs, your rulers, your god, your party, your team, your pet or polar bears, and a ridiculously smart Swedish schoolgirl.
Dichotomy
Dividing into two parts, two concepts, usually in contradiction to one another.
And to really confuse let's consider something that can be both a strength; like eating a family pizza by yourself; and a weakness; eating another family pizza, by yourself.
Dictator
Supreme, absolute authority and power over others within a region.
Dictators are often politicians elected by a majority but who then decide to continue to rule by themselves. They are sometimes surrounded by likeminded idiots calling themselves intellectuals, some of whom also are involuntary food testers. Dictators inspire great respect by wearing stylish uniforms and many impressive bits of metal called medals. Being a dictator ensures eternal fame, awesome wealth and you may be sure that people are not inclined to disagree with you.
Diet
Considered approach to food and drink consumption.
Meat - Kills the environment, the future of our precious children and let's not forget, the animal itself.
Fish - Kills the fish and animals who eat fish, and lakes and oceans.
Plants - Often eaten alive! Plants whom research has now shown to be sentient organisms.
Dingleberry
A small clot of dung, clinging to the backside of a sheep.

In New Zealand and Australia this is a 'dag'. A 'dag' is also slang for an eccentric or entertaining person.

Dingus
An object whose name is unknown or forgotten.
We predict this word will become very much more commonplace to be used as a replacement word for all those we will forget. Without this word you could be quite lost for words.

Diplomacy
The art of dealing with people tactfully.
The ability to win an argument without losing a friend.

Disaster
A calamitous event.
Derived from Latin and Greek this means "bad star". Like the ancients, you could blame the stars (horoscopes) for bad things, but we now know better. Cars and guns are to blame.

Discount
To offer goods or services at a reduced price.
To advertise discounts is always to the financial advantage of all concerned, otherwise it would not happen. The best one seen so far was outside a bar in NZ: Today's special - Buy two Gins of your choice and pay for both.

Distort
To twist out of shape, to misrepresent.
A grimace is distorting your face. The academic field of statistics can be, and often is, employed to distort uncomfortable facts and statisticians are very adept at making insidious truths disappear in convoluted statistics.

Distrust
Lack of trust in, to suspect or doubt.
If your lack of trust is due to knowledge and experience it is distrust, which often is confused with; mistrust, which is due to unease and intuition. As idiots we are generally not troubled by either.

Diversity
Variety; unlike others.
Although most comfort is to be found in being just as stupid as your neighbour, the guiding principle of diversity tells us different species must also be recognised. So, when your neighbour wants to be identified as bobtail cat or a schnauzer then we must afford them the same respect as everyone else. So, when they defecate on the street you do have to pick it up, not ring the police.

Dividend
A share of something to be divided.

A nice word if you get it. If you don't get it then it is a meaningless word.
Docile
Easily taught, trained, managed or obedient.
If one experiences sudden spurts of disobedience, there are medicines for that. Pop a good pill to quickly return to a more comfortable stupor.
Doctor
A person licensed to practice medicine, as a physician, surgeon, dentist, or veterinarian.
It is rewarding to see Doctors are joining the idiotic masses in following orders rather than science. The good thing about this conformist mentality is that if you get sick in a pandemic, or from the vaccines, so will everyone else. Nobody will feel left out.
Document
Any written or printed item, on paper or in a computer, as a book, article, or letter, especially of a factual or informative nature, like a tax declaration, deed or passport.
A document can be a testimony or statement of fact but recently it has been sufficient to cross your fingers behind your back during signing for them to not be upheld by law. This may be regarded as childish but that would be forgetting that every adult also has the right to be childish.
Dormant
In a state of rest, inactivity, or sleep; inoperative; in abeyance.
A suspension of activity often associated with Homer Simpson, teenagers, and volcanoes.
Downsizing
Reducing the number of something, such as employees or participants, usually as a cost-cutting measure.
A phenomenon exclusive to private enterprise. The most useful strategy is to seek employment with government as job security is more important than productivity.
Doublespeak
Evasive or ambiguous language intended to deceive or confuse.
An obsolete word as deceptive language has become the new normal and nobody expects anything truthful from anybody with a public platform.
Drama
Any situation or series of events having emotional, conflicting or striking interest or results.

Apart from transatlantic drama with a king and a ridiculous duke and his beleaguered duchess, high drama is generally associated with political discourse or daytime soap operas. Everyone enjoys other people's dramas more than their own.

Dream
A succession of thoughts, images or emotions passing through the mind during sleep.
It is important to realise that a dream is not reality.
A dream can happen anytime when your eyes are closed and it is where you often do very, very bad things only to wake up and realise you have done something much worse. Fortunately, most dreams don't involve smells.

Drinking
To imbibe or consume a liquid.
Increasingly used to express the consumption of alcohol. Alcohol is loved by many and has many subjective consequences such as you dance better, you see double and feel single. The objective consequences are a little less flattering.

Drone
An unmanned autonomous or remote-controlled flying object used in espionage, warfare and filming the neighbour from above.
The most drastic effect of the popularity of drones is that professional pilots are no longer dapper, well-groomed and well respected in society. Any idiot can now be a pilot and the dress code is greasy sandals, a baseball cap and a wispy beard. The same dress code applies for male pilots. No discrimination.

Drugs
Any substance, illicit or not, other than food, intended to affect the structure or any function of the body of humans or other animals.
They come from your doctor or pharmacist, or they come from a cartel, a peddler, a dealer, a coffee shop or a liquor store. It's all about lines. Fall in line, don't cross the line. The biggest lesson is; know where your laptop is.

Dumb
Lacking intelligence or good judgement.
"Never underestimate the power of stupid people in large groups"
George Carlin.
When large groups of dumb people organise themselves collectively and vote, that is evidence of how wonderful the democratic system is. Who says that, just because there are many more dumb people, they shouldn't have a say. Not stupid people, that's for sure.

Ɛ - 31
Economy
Management of resources.
As we all know this is synonymous with managing to spend. Resources are all well and good and are available from your government, but as every idiot knows, resources have no actual value until we spend them on pet grooming, a footbath from China or a box of fine vintage sherry.
Education
Acquiring or imparting knowledge and developing powers of reasoning and judgement.
Everybody should have the same quality education, and this is the reason why, thankfully, the state wants to, and insist on, controlling it. Thus, we learn how to sit, be quiet, obey and fetch. The view of the state is that we can't have people learning different things because that will lead to complete chaos. People must become useful idiots who can read signs and follow the government's laws and regulations as this encourages us all to live in collective, egalitarian harmony.
Elderly
Of advanced age; old, senior citizen.
If you live a long life, you are first and foremost very lucky and now that you are free to admit that growing up is different to growing old you can terrify people with your driving or say outrageously true things.
Election
A ritual of selection, by voting, of a trustworthy person or persons to represent your views and preferences.
You may castigate your elected officials but eventually you will have an opportunity to castigate other elected officials. Elections therefore, ensures that we always have someone to castigate.
Emotion
Any of the feelings of joy, sorrow, fear, hate, love, jealousy, anger, etc.
It is doubtful previous generations had any emotions at all. Nothing seemed to have disturbed them much. In 21st century western civilisation we have come to recognise the reliably superior idea that our feelings are key to understanding the world around us. The notion that mental toughness and stoicism has any value in an advanced society is ludicrous. All that matters to be taken seriously now is to be aware of the many ways in which the system is victimising us and then announce it publicly. You can talk, with emotion, about your humble beginnings in a violence ridden suburb somewhere, or how you are angry about having been subjected to passive smoke on a bus in 1987 or how you feel wronged about having been in the wrong body your whole life.

Empathy
The sympathetic understanding, and identification, with the feelings of another.
One of the key attributes of an emotionally intelligent human being. As always, intelligence of any kind is overrated and nothing to brag about. When you have embraced ignorance and idleness you can enjoy immunity from emotions in a more natural way.

Empire
A group of nations or peoples ruled by an emperor, empress, or other powerful individual(s).
Eau de toilette by Trump.
Individuals build empires but empires fall by themselves. Like most negative outcomes, they are rarely blamed on those responsible. This is why there is nobody around to ensure we don't make the same mistakes again.

Employee
A person working for another person or a business for payment.
We should all reel at the utter unfairness of such an arrangement. Nobody should have to work for anyone else and those that do so willingly should try to embrace stupidity immediately. Don't they realise that you get free money for doing nothing and that doing nothing isn't very expensive. The foolishness of it all is staggering.

Enema
Liquid injection in the rear.
The end result from an enema may be similar from meeting an enemy. See below.

Enemy
An adversary, opponent, or foe as in individual or state.
There are a great many ways you can treat your enemy; Love your enemy said Jesus. Don't interrupt your enemy, said Napoleon. Become your enemy, said Sun Tzu. Don't be like your enemy, said Marcus Aurelius. Make your enemy your friend, said Abraham Lincoln. Forgive, but never forget your enemy, said John F. Kennedy. Eat your enemy, wrote Shakespeare.
"With friends like you, who needs enemies", Anonymous.
Apart from Shakespeare nobody really thinks an enemy is such a bad apple. Shakespeare however, thought it appropriate to consume the enemy. Like you would an apple.

Entitlement
A provision, amount, advantage, to which one is entitled, a right.
There are two parts to this equation. First, money is taken from those who achieve and then it is given it to those who don't achieve.

Entrepreneur
A person who invests his own time, effort and money on a venture which may or may not be successful.
Who do these people think they are? They expect to profit from others and enslave their workers. If their business is successful, they actually owe it to their employees but never give them adequate compensation for their work. If the entrepreneur fails that just shows us what folly it is to think that you can do something better than someone else.

Environment
Surrounding things, conditions, or influences. Our milieu.
Mostly discussed in terms of the harm that we, human idiots, inflict on it. Upon reflection however we, human idiots, are more likely and more adept at inflicting harm on ourselves. The environment will undoubtedly survive us, human idiots, and we will be among the more than 99% of all species already extinct. Problem solved.

Environmentalism
Absolute submission to Al Gore.
Environmentalism is more compelling than many other religions. We do not tolerate dissent and criticising the religion is an act of blasphemy and is, or soon will be, a crime which in many places is punishable by complete cancellation and will invoke public pillorying.

Evidence
Proves or disproves something; ground for belief; proof.
Proof is generally to be found in puddings. Beware of red herring flavoured puddings.

Equality
The state or quality of being equal.
We are all equal. Never forget though, that some people are more equal than others.
This is reflected in the fact that we are all idiots, but some are bigger idiots than others.
Disparities have existed in the past, but they are rapidly disappearing. Rich and poor, talented, and dull, powerful and powerless, informed and ignorant, male and female, black and white, boy and girl, manager and worker, husband and wife. These divisive terms are all being eradicated, and the world will be greatly improved when we are all the same.

Equity
Something that is made fair and just by unequal treatment.
This word is causing a lot of unnecessary confusion. It essentially means that if the goal is to achieve greater equality, the strategy and

means to achieve this end are unimportant. Anything is permissible, legitimate and even virtuous. So for instance, a fantastic way to achieve a fairer society is to lift all homeless people out of poverty and let them move in with the stars of Hollywood movies. There isn't a single movie star or movie producer who would object to sharing their spacious mansions with those in need because all of them understand equity better than everyone else.

Escalate
To increase in magnitude and intensity.
This is a word which is increasingly ignored in favour of justifiable retribution. If someone is punched in the nose now that justifies the annihilation of that perpetrator's entire family. If someone forgets to wear a seatbelt for two minutes that results in a $1000 fine.

Ethics
Moral principles and values that guide your actions and choices.
Only an individual has an ethical framework. A group is an abstract consisting of individuals and cannot act independent of the individuals within it. Only individuals act. Haha, nearly tricked you. Obsolete nonsense. Of course a group of people can act. Just consider the National Socialists of the 1940's and all the people who voted them in.

Euphemism
Substituting offensive, harsh or blunt language with something more indirect or vague.
Ex. A large cardboard box can euphemistically be described as an environmentally sustainable, transportable, biodegradable, single occupancy dwelling.
Mainstream news outlets increasingly employ the use of lovely euphemisms to avoid harsh realities and obversely; divisive and nasty euphemisms to avoid reporting harmless or benign activities.

Excess
Super abundant or beyond plentiful. Above or more than necessary, permitted, or desirable.
Noise, flatulence, creativity, and sweating are negative examples.
Positive examples include taxation, compliance, and conformity.

Excuse
An apology or justification for indulgence, or to seek to remove blame.
When you open the freezer compulsively, believing that it is a portal to another planet. It isn't, so you have some ice cream.

Evangelical
Zealous and ardent support and enthusiasm for a cause. Can pertain to Christian gospel.

When you find that parking spot or when your toast lands the right way up you know that it was a miracle. When you stub your toe or relieve yourself in the laundry basket in the dark, that was not quite a miracle, it was inevitable.

Evil
Morally wrong; bad; wicked.
One must never forget that if you vote for a lesser evil, you are still voting for evil. But because you are a knob you are allowed and even encouraged to forget this.

Exam
A test to show the knowledge and ability of a student.
No idiot likes exams. You would have to be extra stupid to like them. Tip: If you write your exam with your non-dominant hand then it feels like someone else is destroying your future.

Example
Something illustrating a general rule.
'For example,' 'case in point' and 'for instance' may not be proof of anything but remains worthwhile tools to shut down opposing views, particularly if you raise your voice.

Execution
The act of inflicting effective destructive action and/or capital punishment.
In a functioning civilisation we must entrust our leaders and the state to execute people. No individual would generally want to, or know how to, do it and those that try are always described as criminals and go to jail. When our elected rulers execute people, or things, they get medals and book deals and the media calls them heroic.

Explain
To make plain, interpret or clarify.
If you are stupid you will accept any explanation. If you are smart you will accept no explanation.

Exploit
A notable deed or heroic act. Also, accomplishment.
Ok, settle down. Nothing is as rewarding as relaxation, leisure, and inactivity.

Exploited
Used selfishly by someone for their own sends.
We have all experienced being exploited. This is why we are all victims. The world is a terrible place, and everything is awful and now it is worse than ever. Everyone knows it. An idiot called me an idiot yesterday. At least we are not alone.

Extortion
The crime of obtaining cash or advantage by abusing one's position or authority.
Not actually a crime if the state does it. It is a healthy thing to extort money from those that earn more to give to those that earn less. This is what is called equity. Treating everyone differently for the purpose of eliminating differences. We should help the state in this noble cause.
See Looting.

ف - 36

Fabianism
Socialists advocating for gradual rather than revolutionary economic reform.
According to the internet Fabian is a blobfish. Real Fabianism however, is way too slow for most idiots. Socialism must come about much faster. Stalin had some great ideas but of course, that wasn't real socialism.
We will do better. We know better.

Fable
A short tale or anecdote, not founded on facts, to teach a moral lesson, often with animals or inanimate objects as characters.
'The boy who cried Wolf' is a well-known fable. Lesser known are 'The Weasel got the most Votes' and 'The Business of Monkey Business'.

Face
The front part of your head which has a variety of individual features showing a range of expressions.
For various reasons, mainly attributable to conformity or submissiveness, we sometimes choose to cover our faces with masks. This activity hides the face, which for some, has been a welcome cultural change. Perhaps not as welcome as with those who would otherwise have to see that same face.

Fact
Something that actually exists, reality, truth.
Facts are mostly unreliable and should always be regarded by good citizens as suspicious and if any confirmation of veracity is required, please refer to knowledgeable authorities on the matter. The fact is that we know nothing for certain and we know this for a fact.
Books can often mislead and should be avoided or burned, or both.

Faith
Complete trust.

The only way to access reality is through faith. You must believe in what you are told. You must trust CNN or the New York Times, or both. Conviction is more important than truth.

Fallacy
A false notion or belief.
Basing an argument on a fallacy requires that you choose a good fallacy. Beware of false fallacies. Do a factcheck with a reputable source such as BBC or CNN.

Family
A family is a group of two or more persons related by birth, marriage, or adoption who live together.
A family is far less important than the state whom you can always rely upon to look after you, educate you, feed you, house you, entertain you and treat you with dignity. In progressive Sweden 85.4% of children from age 1 to 5 are in state controlled childcare facilities. They have also outlawed homeschooling. That is positive progress.

Fanaticism
Extreme, unquestioning devotion and zeal in support of an ideology, a party, religion, or cause.
Mindless allegiance to the cause of mindlessness will ensure a blissful, peaceful existence without being subjected to the trauma of choice.

Fart
A release of intestinal gas through the anus. A flatus.
We used to cover a fart with a discreet cough but since the covid pandemic we fart to cover a cough. And no, it's not aerosolised protein, nor is it caused by pulling a digit.

Fascism
A governmental system led by a dictator together with an oligarchy or corporate elite, having complete power, forcibly suppressing opposition and criticism, controlling, or regimenting all production, commerce, etc., and often emphasizing or supporting tribalism and racism. Also known as corporatism.
The linguistic distinctions have been blurred to the extent that the word antifascism is now synonymous with fascism. In this way every idiot can protest about almost anything and as confusion rules, the biggest idiots of all, those in the ruling elite, have more freedom to do what they do best, to provide for us all using rich people's money.

Feelings
A self-contained phenomenal experience.
My feelings don't care about your facts. That is because your facts are yours and they have nothing to do with me. I have my own.

Female
Relating to a man or woman or girl or boy with a certain combination of sex characteristics including two X chromosomes, a vagina, a uterus and ovaries, and enlarged breasts developed at puberty.
According to one of the biggest idiots in our society, a supreme court justice, it is impossible to assign a gender unless you are a biologist, and this undoubtedly includes your own gender. The question then arises: how can anyone be unhappy with their own gender until they have been told what their gender is?
Feminism
A doctrine empowering women to realise equal rights with men.
Much of this relates to banishing old-fashioned words containing 'man' and these must be desexed and made more inclusive. Examples of unacceptable words include Mango, Manic, Manage, Manure, Manhole and Many. This dictionary will be updated as these words are replaced.
Fiasco
A complete and utter failure.
A lovely Italian word meaning a really bad bottle made of glass. Perhaps a bottle with two holes instead of one. Or perhaps the hole is at the wrong end.
Fiction
Something invented or imagined, a made-up story. Imaginative literature. Not fact.
True Fiction is confusing as it can't be both. It is just as confusing as other oxymorons like Virtual Reality or Civil War.
Filthy
Completely dirty.
The poor used to sometimes be referred to as filthy beggars, but this is no longer the case. As economic opportunity is being eroded for the middle class, poverty is becoming more inclusive, and these people are usually anything but filthy.
Finish
To complete; bring something to an end.
When you drink with the Finnish you are finished.
Also, when you finish thinking, you are finished.
The alternative is more appealing.
So, it follows that if you don't think, then there is no need to finish.
Flamboyant
Strikingly bold or brilliant; showy. Dashing.
A wonderful word, the meaning of which has been narrowed, now pertaining exclusively to homosexual or transexual behaviour.

Flattery
Insincere or excessive praise.
The oxymoron, pretty ugly, can be pure flattery, well, at least it is more flattering than just ugly or butt ugly, but it will get you nowhere. Politicians are acutely aware that, because of the steep decline of the average intellect, flattery is becoming more effective.

Flummoxed
Confused.
If you thought you knew what this word meant but didn't, this word describes you well.

Flying
Pass through air, with or without wings.
An activity frowned upon as it destroys the environment. As people will soon be prevented from flying, the word is expected to become a linguistic fossil.

Follower
A person who subscribes to, or adheres to, certain ideas or beliefs; or imitates, copies, or takes as a model or ideal.
The groupies, sycophants, bootlickers, or admirers of the world are manifesting the human need for the comfort and security to be found in numbers. People seek out those who gives them absolute answers which then helps to soothe their fears and anxieties.

Fool
A silly or stupid person; a person who lacks judgment or sense. Or a jester.
To describe a fool as a halfwit suggests that half of the wit is still present. It rarely is.

The other definition, however, is more interesting. A jester is a person who, historically at least, plays the fool, wearing a funny cap with bells on it. The jester was more than an entertainer as they also provided the ruler and employer with insight and advice. This made it possible to assign virtues such as honesty and common sense to jesters. In our enlightened time acting in a jester-like fashion is a rare phenomenon as rulers take themselves more seriously and don't see kindly to being made fun of. Off with their heads. Cancel them. A dawn raid does the job.

Football
A game of skill where a ball is generally kicked around by two opposing teams.
In football as well as in many other sports, two teams consent to play under a set of rules which are determined by an independent body. This is not acceptable, and sports should follow the lead of politics and allow the winning team to create new rules or ignore existing ones if they wish to. Maybe they would widen the goals, introduce hate speech penalties, or introduce a sin bin or penalty kicks for overreacting?

Forbid
To make a rule or law against something.
"In Sweden it is forbidden by law to be a criminal" said a previously prominent political leader.
This is why Sweden has no crime. Laws are very effective. More countries should follow suit and make it illegal to break the law.

Force
The physical power or strength possessed by a living being or as exerted on an object. Violence and coercion.
As we choose to define violence as intentionally causing harm to a person, then speech is often violence. As such it must be made illegal to speak without consideration of others and our authorities, with the backing of legacy media are making great strides to prevent uncontrolled speech to ensure that we are safe from violence.

Foreign
Strange or unfamiliar. From another country.
Nothing is strange any longer. If you have a preference for the familiar, then you are a racist and a bigot. Be a good citizen and share all you have with people you don't know. That's what all global leaders do.

Forgive
To grant pardon for; or remission of an offense, debt, etc.; absolve.
Catholics are advantaged having a fast-track system for forgiveness.

Form
The shape of someone or something. To produce or make.
This word is increasingly in use as we fill these in daily.
Forms are an efficient way to organise and control society. There still exists a subset of individuals who fill forms out incorrectly and there must be harsh penalties for such abhorrent, disrespectful behaviour.
Fragment
A part broken off, isolated or detached.
An example of something that is infinitely fragmentable is group identity. You can't support a minority without supporting the smallest minority of all, which is of course, one idiot.
Freedom
Freedom of choice. Free from coercion, authoritarian control, bondage, or slavery.
A silly old word which is gradually becoming obsolete. Freedom is a real problem in today's world as it must be regulated to a high degree to protect idiots from themselves. The only context in which the word is positive is when referring to free food, free shelter, free healthcare, free education and free public transport. As any idiot knows, none of those things can be provided without the state enforcing taxation of the rich so that it can be paid for.
Having said that, freedom can be experienced when removing very tight undergarments.
Freeway
Motorway free of intersections.
Nothing is free about this kind of road as it is very expensive. This is aptly illustrated with the expression highway robbery.
A freeway is perfectly suited for protesting freeways.
See *Protest.*
Frivolous
Self-indulgently carefree; unconcerned about or completely lacking any serious purpose.
A word often used to describe certain lawsuits, most of them unsuccessful. Such as a high school student who sued for being woken up in class, or a kidnapper who sued his hostages for escaping.
Frugal
Economical in using or in spending; prudently saving or sparing; not wasteful. Thrifty.
People are increasingly becoming proud of living is caves and eating roadkill and insects. They call it 'preparing', and every idiot should familiarise themselves with frugal living because the day will come when we are all equal, in poverty.

Fruit
A useful plant part of which may be edible.
How the English language has evolved is not always obvious, but convention has it that some fruits are called fruits; like jackfruit, dragon fruit and passionfruit. Without the fruit they would be Jack, dragon, and passion. Grape is a fruit either way, but also different.

Fuddle
To muddle or confuse.
I.E. The same as befuddle but with the excuse of alcohol intoxication.

G – 24

Gambling
To stake or risk money, or anything of value, on the outcome of something involving chance.
Chances are you should have quit while you were ahead but if you have a chronic gambling addiction problem, the bet is that it is difficult to come out a winner.
In fact, the odds are not in your favour at all. But an idiot would still put money on it.

Gender
Either the male or female division or binary classification of a species, especially as differentiated by social and cultural roles and behaviour.
An outrageously out of date definition as it is widely recognised that there are at least seventy but maybe even a thousand different genders. According to a Supreme Court Justice in the U.S. it is not possible to identify a gender unless a biologist does so, and this naturally includes your own gender. This has not been obvious to everyone before, but it is now. Do not assume. You do not know.

Generation
The entire group of people who are of a similar age and whom have similar attributes, problems and values.
Silent, Boomers, X, Millennials and Z. It is the role of older generations to continue to victimise young people and make them angry, poor, destitute, stupid, and incompetent. But they too will grow up and continue to victimise their own offspring.

Generosity
Liberal giving or sharing.
The emphasis is on an individual being generous which entails freely giving of our own resources as opposed to the socialistic approach of generously redistributing the resources of everybody but yourself.
Liberal in the sense of enabling the sharing of the abundant resources of others. Giving of your own time and resources is unnecessary since others have so much more to give.

See *Stupid.*
Genius
A person with exceptional natural capacity of intellect, especially as shown in creative and original work in science, art, music, etc.
Unless spelled Jenius it refers to an individual with an IQ over 140. Recently however, it has become perfectly acceptable to self-identify as a genius, regardless of whether you can reason, read an analogue clock, or remember how to pronounce your own name, Kamala.
Gentleman
A chivalrous, courteous, or honourable man and referred to as such. A man embodying discretion, restraint, and integrity.
A person overtly obsessed with banal things like punctuality and personal hygiene. No wonder then that this pompous tradition is completely out of fashion. It is also a non-inclusive, sexist word which has its uses as an incivility until inevitably it becomes obsolete.
German
A people most famous for drinking beer and eating sausages.
Germans do have a sense of humour but just like their language, you must know it before you understand it. I mean, with a word like krankenwagen, wow. Germans are not angry, they are German.
Gin
An alcoholic liquor originally made in Salerno, Italy with distilled grain spirit flavoured with juniper berries.
A delicious spirit which has a colourful past. At one point, hundreds of years ago, juniper was in short supply and was substituted with turpentine. Gin has also been used to treat fear, gallstones and gout and it has been the cause of several riots. A classic Martini is made with Gin, never with Vodka, which is why that James Bond guy must explain himself every time.
Girl
A female child.
A soon to be obsolete term for a young female. Likely to be replaced with; 'a small person with eggs in it.'
See *Female.*
Glass
A hard, transparent, crystalline substance used to make bottles and windows etc.
There are great many cracking jokes about glass, but did you also know that glass is neither a liquid nor a solid. Just another idiotic fact.
Globalisation
Extending to other countries or the whole world.

Relating to cross-border trade, travel and sharing of information. Globalisation makes it possible to for Eskimos to eat pineapples and for Bedouins to drive Ferraris.

Globalism
The attitude and policy of placing the interests of the entire world above those of individual nations.
Globalism is a political ideology displacing a nations interest in favour of universally desirable outcomes. We are supremely fortunate that the supersized genius of Klaus Swab and other towering intellectuals in charge hold our collective interest so close to heart as they feed us more insects and reduce poverty in places like Sri Lanka. We must ensure they have all possible support from all us idiots to "Master the Future". Not that much support is needed. We don't even have to vote for them.
See *Media*.

Gluten
A gluey substance generally found in glue or grain products.
It may be possible to eat gluten-free food without telling everyone, but it is yet to be proven.

Good
Morally superior, virtuous; pious
Humans are so very bad that it is not safe to let us have freedom of choice. Luckily, we have politicians and bureaucrats who organise our lives for us and since they are good instead of bad, they alone can be trusted in all that they do.

Goodness
Kindness, generosity, high morals, virtuous.
Do-gooders do so much good. Especially if they work for or represent the state. There they do much good for themselves and others and they don't even have to spend their own money to do so.

Government
A political elite ruling by threats and coercion. I.E. Laws and edicts.
Virtuous individuals employed by government to find ways to stop non-government individuals from making money and enjoying themselves.
See *Greed* and *Collectivism*.

Gratitude
Feeling or being thankful.
You were never consulted on whether you wanted to be born or live the life you have so there is no reason you should feel any gratitude for being here. In fact, a growing number of people are litigating against their parents for this lack of consideration. Justice will prevail.

Greed
Intense and selfish desire, especially for wealth or possessions.
Non-government individuals making money and enjoying themselves, at the expense of all workers.
See *Government.*

Green
The verdant colour of growing foliage, between yellow and blue in the spectrum.
The colour adopted by a political movement whose adherents are more likely to consume growing foliage than others. This may be slightly ironic since green politicians are the self-proclaimed protectors of the environment. But it has been said, brown is the new green.

Growth
Gradual increase; development.
The larger the government grows the fewer problems we seem to have. If everyone worked for the government, there would be no problems at all.

Guilt
The feeling of responsibility or remorse for some offense, crime, wrong, whether real or imagined. Culpability, or having violated a moral or penal law.
The best way to never be judged or feel guilt is to never admit guilt. 'The dog did it' or it was an 'administrative error' or better still, ignoring the accusation completely will render the guilt unconvincing at worst and forgotten at best.

Gulag
The system of forced-labour camps in the Soviet Union.
A remote place of residence for persons unable to accept that Socialism in all its forms is the way of the future. The Gulag archipelago may have been characterised as lacking some luxuries, but it did offer re-education and work opportunities were abundant. Tipping was not expected.

Gun
Any portable firearm, or a dispensing tool for hot glue.
Many idiots claim that guns kill people and therefore must be banned. My computer, which incidentally writes these words independent of me, agrees. The sad thing is that not only are guns killing people but so are snakes, ladders, batteries, and bathtubs. We should ban all of them without delay, that would be the idiotic approach.

Guru
An intellectual or spiritual guide or leader.
Absolutely not a phoney.

H – 21
Habit
A behaviour pattern regularly followed until it becomes involuntary.
Hard work can become a habit, but thankfully, so can laziness.
Handouts
Anything given away costing you nothing.
If you feel dumb enough to want to be elected to public office, promising handouts of other people's money is an effective strategy to create revenue and gain enough votes so that you can seize power over other people's lives.
Happiness
Good fortune; pleasure; contentment; joy, and delight.
The key to happiness varies. For some, ruining the happiness of others makes them very happy. For others, happiness is a certain hour or finding a matching sock.
Hazard
Something that is, or can cause, unavoidable danger, peril, risk, or difficulty.
Stupidity is regarded as hazardous by some, but in reality intelligence is far more dangerous. Take Einstein for instance. Clever guy, right? Thanks to him, at least indirectly, we now have weapons that can destroy our species. Had he been an idiot, the world might be quite different now. Red buttons might not have been invented.
Health
The general condition of the body or mind with reference to soundness, vitality, and vigour.
It is indeed great that we can rely on public health experts with WHO and pharmaceutical companies to care for us and keep us alive and healthy. Like every idiot in existence, we understand that we owe our lives to the politicians in charge of the public health organisations.
Heartless
Unsympathetic and unkind; harsh; cruel.
A person who objects to their money being spent to buy votes.
Help
To provide what is necessary to accomplish a task or satisfy a need.
We need lots of help and getting it used to mean waiting in line and getting coughed on or, listening to endless distorted music before being allowed to speak with a robot which hangs up on you, or downloading an app that doesn't let you do anything at all, but these days government services are exceptionally efficient and never lets us down.
Hero
A person noted for courageous acts or nobility of character.

"It was absolutely involuntary. They sank my boat." John F. Kennedy on becoming a war hero.
A hero acts with no thought of personal gain or glory. To think, or regularly speak, of personal gain or glory makes you a politician, not a hero.

History
A continuous and systematic narrative of past events as relating to a particular people, country, period, or person.
History is a record. And records are meant to be broken. History used to be an effective way to learn about past mistakes and how we can avoid making them again. Fortunately, we can now safely ignore our past as we are told that it was a cauldron of dystopian backwardness and bigotry. Idiots all around the world now live in different, more rational times and we must make our own mistakes because, as we are so much more advanced, our mistakes will be bigger and better, so they will require new, enlightened solutions.

Homicide
The killing of a human being by another.
Some special people can kill another person, or even lots of people, simply by snapping his or her fingers. The people performing the actual homicides aren't murderers. They are following orders and are just doing their job.

Honesty
Being truthful, sincere, frank.
Honesty is well recognised to be criminally harmful, and we know lies can be socially responsible and extremely useful. Every idiot lies.

Hope
The feeling that what is wanted can be had or that outcomes can be achieved.
An incredibly useful and emotive word used to rally support for any cause or politician. As it is an abstract term it eliminates the need for concrete obligations and contractual commitments with performance metrics and potential penalties. Hoping for the impossible doesn't make it any more possible.

Hopeless
Despair. Impossible to accomplish, solve, resolve, etc.
"I am a hopeless addict... because I forget to feed my addictions" Jonas.
This word is useful as it justifies inaction and passivity.
It also a word used as justification for soliciting funds from those that don't deserve them.

Horror
Intense fear or dread.
The overwhelming feeling of helplessness you have just before discovering that the World Economic Forum has our back and that all will be well. If we could vote for Klaus Swab, we would.
Hospital
An institution and/or building in which sick or injured people are given medical or surgical treatment. Or a similar establishment for the care of animals.
The general activities include connecting people to beeping things and when the beeping stops, they are no longer sick.
Hubris
Excessive pride or dangerous over-confidence; boundless arrogance.
Hubris is the delusional condition affecting idiots in leadership roles making them think they are God. It is the cause of much suffering but as idiots we know that the suffering will always affect somebody else, unless of course we deserve to suffer. Which we probably do.
Human
Relating to beings identifying as human.
As a minority among species, we enjoy special privileges. Chief among them is to control other species to benefit ours.
Humanity
An abstract, collective term for all humans, the human race. Also, the quality of being humane, kind, and benevolent.
Humanism has led to much inhumanity but that can be attributed to a misinterpretation of the word. Much evil is done in the name of humanity when, in reality, only a small number of individuals are ultimately responsible, and their henchwomen and henchmen of course. Fortunately, this never happens in democracies.
Hypocrisy
Having a virtuous character, moral or religious beliefs or principles that one does not really possess.
The idea that laws only apply to thee but not me runs deep in most cultures. Children see it better than fully grown adults. When you tell a child that it is wrong to steal a chocolate bar but it's absolutely fine to loot a store or even coerce money from a worker in the form of taxation, then the child might be a little confused but as the child grows into a fully grown idiot this will all become crystal clear.
Hypocrite
A person who acts in contradiction to stated beliefs or principles.
The beautiful thing about principles is that they are as flexible as beliefs, or even feelings. We must not limit ourselves in terms of

having any fixed values or ideas that cannot be changed when exposed to other, superior, facts from our leaders or media for instance.
Hysterical
Irrationally emotional.
This chaotic emotional response is most profoundly caused by understanding how the world actually works and realising how you are nearly powerless to affect any change. Better then to join a herd of numbskulls and forget about it. There is so much more joy in that.

J – 39
Idea
Any thought, notion or conception existing in the mind as a result of mental understanding, awareness, or activity.
Our politicians and thought leaders understand and live according to the principle that a bad idea is superior to no idea. So, they have some ideas, but are they good ideas? They have no idea.
Identity
The state or fact of being oneself or itself, and not another.
In the past, something you chose to identify with, which was not based in fact, was not something you were. Linguistic and ideological evolution has resulted in such archaic notions being rejected.
Objectively determining someone's identity is now only done by intolerant, fact denying bigots. Modern facts are much improved.
Idealism
The cherishing of ideas and perceptions of things as they should be.
Reality can never overpower idealism. Ignorance can.
Ideology
The body of doctrine, myth, belief, etc., that guides and activates an individual, a social movement, an institution, a class, or a large group.
Safety and comfort can be found in belonging to a larger collective of likeminded ideologues. The larger, or more violent the minority grows, the more power it has, until of course it becomes a majority, then it is time to reimagine words or divide the minority into further subsets of people.
Identification
Something that identifies a person.
Identifying an idiot isn't as straightforward as you might think. They don't always have dribble on their chin or a vacant expression in their eyes. Many of the most prominent idiots wear suits and ties and are usually found either giving or following orders and hilariously, they nearly always think they are smarter than you.
Idiot
An utterly foolish or senseless person.

A great way to be as life is tremendously simple. Idiot politicians and idiot bureaucrats look after us and nobody pressures us into doing strenuous things like thinking and working.

Many bureaucrats stupidly try to make things completely idiot proof, but we just get betterer at it. You can't fool an idiot. We are foolproof.

Idiots
A gaggle of morons.
We set out to write this book on idiots, but we found it was easier to write it on paper.
Idiots are now the majority. This is why we should be grateful for democracy. Idiots rule the world. Democracy is foolproof.

Ignorance
Lack of learning, knowledge, or information.
You too can be, or probably are, ignorant. It is a state of being that does require some commitment but as evidenced by so many devotees within the highest institutions of learning, the commitment to ignorance is escalating and highly fashionable. If you require further evidence just look at Harvard and many other Universities. There are long lines of students willing to pay astronomical fees to become complete idiots.

Imagination
The faculty of imagining, and ability to imagine, or forming mental images of concepts of what is not actually present to the senses.
Anything can be imagined and become your reality. You just need to believe it deeply enough. For instance, imagine that you are smart. That is a smart thing to do, so that made you smart. But being smart is completely unnecessary and may entail a societal backlash. Imagine being an idiot instead. It is less lonely and you will be happier.

Impartial
Unbiased, fair, and just.
Impartiality is determined by asking the question "Are you impartial?". If the answer is "yes", then you have found an impartial person. If, as an example, this person is part of a jury, then he or she or ze or gee or they will contribute to society by helping to convict and incarcerate people who break hate speech laws or wander through public buildings.

Impeachment
To bring an accusation of misconduct against. To call to account.
Unpresidenting actions which further liberates legacy media from outdated, orthodox compliance to truth and integrity. These useful sideshows effectively divert public attention from actual villains. The meaning of the word has changed drastically as the intention of

impeachments are not to impeach but to destroy reputations and control electoral outcomes.
Impossible
Unable to be done, perform, complete, learn, happen etc.
"It is impossible for a man to learn what he thinks he already knows"
Epictetus.
If nothing is impossible, then it follows that it is impossible for anything to be impossible.
 In the interest of equal rights the quote above now also applies to women and all other genders.
Impulse
A sudden, involuntary inclination prompting you to act.
Doing something impulsive is your brain taking positive action to avoid future regret.
Inclusivity
Welcoming, or not excluding members or participants on the basis of gender, race, class, sexuality, disability, etc.
Look at everyone wanting to be different, just like everybody else. You can be anything at this point and you will not be judged. If you want dress in a bell skirt and eat cake with your feet while claiming to be a left-handed ostrich with dyslexia, there is nothing anyone can do to stop you. Certainly not in the English-speaking world. You will have fans and followers, many from Canada.
Inconclusive
Without a result or outcome. Not fully resolving questions or doubts.
An extraordinarily useful term to help you avoid conveying bad news, and to request more funding.
Inconsistent
Different parts or elements in conflict with, or at odds with one another.
Being consistently inconsistent can infuriate others. If someone points out any inconsistency in your arguments or ideology the most powerful counter action is to accuse your opponent of racism, sexism, or bigotry.
Incompetence
A lack of ability to perform or accomplish.
At the peak of incompetence, you will find yourself very content indeed and it is not unusual to gain a promotion at this point. Most importantly please realise that you are never alone. Incompetence is the apex of the human condition.
Indoctrination
To instruct in a doctrine, ideology, or biased belief.

The dominant ideology of our recent past, capitalism, is thankfully being dispensed with in favour of the current and accelerating indoctrination into socialism, which is superior in every way. Any idiot can tell you that our academic institutions are proficient at indoctrination, and we look forward to seeing a brave new world with equality and prosperity for all.

Independence
Freedom from control and influence from others.
'You don't have to anything' is an outdated idea and one which would result in civilizational decline and endless misery. Instead, we must recognise the global political leadership as having achieved superior stupidity and we should continue to comply with every rule, statute and law as they are ensuring harmony and prosperity for all.

Individual
A single human being, as distinguished from a group.
It is well known that the smallest minority is the individual and as such they are the most oppressed of all. Subjective authenticity tells us that this is correct, and wrong. But as groups consisting of many individuals are suffering many more inequalities, it naturally follows that groups are oppressed more than individuals. For example, you belong to the group idiots, which is often treated unfairly, despite being in majority. There are many, many other groups that you may belong to; morons, fools, right-handed, left-handed, left footed, right footed, legless, purple haired, etc.

Individualism
The principle of independent thought or action.
A confusing and very upsetting ideology that selfishly places you in charge of your own life and your own decisions. This idea is a manifestation of privilege and has been refuted repeatedly and beyond choosing what to put on your toast or on your feet, individuals are not capable of making decisions or to think for themselves. This must be done by elected rulers or leaders. They are not individuals.

Individuality
That which distinguishes one individual from another.
In their quest of individuality people naturally gravitate toward conformity. Being different means being singled out and just like every fish knows, safety can be found in numbers.

Indolent
Predisposed to slothfulness and inactivity.
If you are too lazy to write a book on how to be lazy, this is you. The main symptom of indolence is

Infamy
Bad reputation as a result of a shameful, criminal, or outrageous act.
"Infamy, infamy, they've all got it in for me" - said not Julius Caesar. It is an all but impossible achievement to be infamous and you can even expect to become a President of the United States before you will achieve the status of infamy.

Infantile
The characteristic of or befitting an infant.
It is childish to claim you are not childish or stupid. The same is true for words like sophomoric and infantile.
These terms are closely related to 'idiot'. Not one adult will believe you if you make the assertion that you are not an idiot.

Infinity
See *Loop*.

Information
Knowledge, including news; gained, communicated, or received.
There is actually no need to learn anything, not even reading. as audiobooks and videos explain everything. All the information we will ever need is on our phones.

Inflation
To increase the volume of money in circulation which results in the loss of value of currency and price increases.
The objective of this deliberate action is to move the ends so that they never meet. The person to blame for such nefarious activities is of course, Vladimir.

Influence
Compel force on, or produce effects on the actions, behaviour, or opinions of others.
Lemmings, reindeer and young people are easily influenced. Like the murmurings of starlings, any individual finding themselves left behind the collective panics and has to seek therapy or take medication.

Insanity
Being deranged or foolish of mind.
The identification of the insane is made by the less insane. Insanity generally has a more negative effect on those who claim they are not.

Insidious
Beguiling but harmful and deceitful.
The powerful using fear of any bogeyman or bogeywoman imaginable, including your neighbour, to scare you into compliance and accepting anything at all, including staying in your apartment and covering your face. As it turns out, not really that harmful though, is it?

Insolence
Contemptuously rude behaviour or speech; brazen.
A degree of comprehension is not a prerequisite for insolence. Sophomoric ignorance and bloated arrogance are.
Institution
An organisation founded for a religious, educational, professional, or social purpose. An established practise.
Being committed to an institution is very different from committing to an institution. The first could be imprisonment and the second could be a marriage. Oh..., perhaps not that different, for some.
Insurance
A contract in which one party agrees to indemnify or reimburse another for loss that occurs under the terms of the contract.
The only drawback with being an idiot and that is that your insurance does not cover accidental injury caused by stupidity. Being an idiot is a pre-existing condition so if you swallow brake fluid, kick a crocodile, or drive with your eyes shut, the insurance is voided.
Intellect
Faculty for thinking; mental capacity.
Demonstrably unnecessary as evidenced by Kamala Harris who has shown that brazen stupidity is perfectly acceptable for leadership roles.
Intelligence
The faculty of understanding.
The population is often described as being a lot smarter than they are given credit for. This is pandering to a diminishing minority and disrespects the idea that we are very proud of our ignorance. Being an idiot is not something to be embarrassed about and if our leaders were clever, which they are not, they would be ashamed of their imbecility. Intelligence will soon be replaced by artificial intelligence.
Artificial, without intelligence, has also been shown to be effective as it can elevate you to a Vice Presidents post.
Intolerance
Unwillingness or refusal to tolerate or respect opinions or beliefs contrary to one's own.
Showing intolerance is a great way to demonstrate that you are intolerant of other idiots' intolerance. Let us be honest, it is conformity of opinion which offers the best solution for a harmonious society so let us all be idiots and conform to the majority views of the world, or maybe that should be some other majority, like race, or region or something else. Maybe we should vote on it?
Invasion
Entering as an enemy.

Invading someone's space, privacy, or country is a virtuous act when the reason for doing so is to spread democracy or minimise harm. Property rights are going out of fashion in any case.

Islam
Absolute submission to Allah.
Islam, the faith of Muslims, is an all-inclusive religious system which asserts all criticism of it is profane and will incur severe penalties, including death. This effectively eliminates criticism.

Jail
An institution for incarcerating or confining people accused or convicted of a crime.
Less long term than a prison which in turn is a word that has been replaced with 'custodial correctional facility'.
A popular location for those idiots who don't like paying bills and who crave discipline and stability.

Jealousy
Feeling threatened by, or resentment against a rival, a person enjoying success or advantage, etc., or against another's success or advantage itself.
The malicious version of envy. If yawn was a girl's name every man could die at 7.00am.

Job
A task, or full or part time employment.
A job is easy to get if you have experience. Experience is easy to get if you have a job.
This may seem problematic, but only if you think a job is worth having. Government will pay you not to have a job. The amount you receive for not working may not seem enough to live on but that is wrong. Governments would never allow you to starve or sleep rough. In any case, soon there will be many more people without jobs so we can, collectively, vote for those who give us the most without having to work.

Journalist
A collector, recorder, interpreter, writer, distorter and distributor of news and daily events.
A professional journalist earns his keep creating or conveying information for the feebleminded. Idiots love media simplifying world events and reinforcing the power and authority of our leaders. Where would we be without all these great journalists? We would be lost, confused, forced to think for ourselves and confronted with too many hard choices.

Judge
A person appointed or elected to determine outcomes and dispense justice according to the law. An arbiter of truth.
If you find yourself having to appear in front of a judge you may want to consider a name change first. Innocent is a practical name.

Jury
A group selected according to law and sworn to determine the facts concerning a case or an accusation submitted to them and to render a verdict to a court.
With an idiot presiding and idiots judging an idiot who is represented by another idiot makes for an interesting spectacle. As we are meant to be judged by our peers it is important that everyone in the courtroom is equally stupid.

𝒦 - 3

Karen
A female name.
This word is commonly used to describe an entitled, obnoxious person prone to irrational behaviour, a person who really should calm down and embrace their stupidity and wear a mask like the rest of us idiots. The male equivalent is either Chad or Kevin.

Kindness
Charity, generosity, compassion, benevolence to yourself and others.
Kindness, like smiling, can be very contagious. But, where random acts of kindness are inspiring, smiling randomly is just creepy.

Knowledge
Investigation or study of facts, truths or principles of a subject.
Gaining knowledge is about digging deeper into a subject, not wider. There is no point considering worldviews opposite to your own as there is plenty to learn which conforms to your opinions. Better to be sure than be right. Being right is always wrong anyway. Too right.

ℒ - 28

Lackadaisical
Lacking enthusiasm, interest, or energy; indolent or sluggish.
A tremendously useful and rewarding approach to life which has nothing at all to do with a shortage of flowers and everything to with spiritual and physical contentment.

Land
Any part of the surface of our planet not covered by water.
"In the land of the blind, the one-eyed man is king" English proverb.

Land represents abundance in all things, opportunity, life, energy, sustenance, and beauty. We must slow down, leave it alone and treat it with care and respect, and compared with water, we do.

Language
A body of words and the systems for their use common to a people who share the same community or nation, the same geographical area, or the same cultural tradition.
Another way for us to feel as though we belong to a collective. This time through using one of thousands of languages. But as all aspiring idiots we know the mangling of language and the constant changing words present a massive challenge to communication. Fortunately, this is made so much simpler when you can refer to an effective and honest dictionary such as the one in your hand.

Law
Rules as created by nature or by government. The breach or violation of either will result in negative consequences.
"Good people do not need laws to tell them to act responsibly, while bad people will find a way around the laws" Plato.
Laws are instituted so that everyone may live at the expense of everyone else. This is especially true for those who write the laws. This makes more sense than sense itself. Laws also help in creating crime and criminals.

Lawyer
Represent a client in a court of law. Act or advise clients in other legal matters.
It is sometimes said that it is the majority of lawyers who give the rest a bad name.
The sheer number of laws in existence with many more on the way makes this a fast-growing profession and these days it is not uncommon for lawyer's lawyers to have lawyers. You can understand why a dentist would need a dentist, but did you ever hear of a plumber needing a plumber? No. They can't afford one. Lawyers can.

Laziness
Sluggish idleness or unwillingness to work.
We can all be quite successful at this which is the main attraction, and it also makes perfect sense to rest before you get tired.

Leader
A person leading or guiding.
You can lead from behind with a loud voice (generals and parents); from the front by example (tour guides and small business owners); from the top by decree and compulsion (political leaders and drug lords) or not all (bureaucrats and workers). All are idiots, some are just

more important idiots than others. As we are destined to be equal this situation is being addressed and rectified by our biggest idiots, the political elite.

Learn
To acquire knowledge of, or skill in, by study, instruction, or experience.
"Rarely is the questioned asked: Is our children learning?" George W. Bush.
The key rule is that you can't be bad at something you haven't learnt. Don't learn - Do no wrong. Not bad.

Lecture
A rebuke or reprimand. Also, something like an instruction given to students.
The louder the reprimand, the easier it is to hear. That much is obvious.
It is voluntary to listen to lectures which is good because being talked down to is unacceptable, especially since we are all equal. More equal than ever before and more than anyone else.

Left
Belonging to the political left, having liberal and/or radical views.
Idiots everywhere want to belong and not be left out. Being on the political left ensures you are part of a popular and strident ideology driven by a need to redistribute wealth and power, guided by Marxist ideas, and striving for equality in every facet of life. The rhetoric is attractive, never mind that the process being somewhat compulsive in nature. Fortunately, laws of economics, human nature or truths of political philosophy need not be obstacles when you realise objective truth does not exist.

Legacy
Something handed down from the past or how we are remembered long after we are gone.
'Seriously! A bloody salad?' - Julius Caesar.
Adolf Hitler Beetle - Blind Slovenian Cave Beetle.

Legal
Permitted by law, lawful.
The legal system is created by idiots to authorise taking from some to give to others, including themselves. This moral activity is glorified in the name of equity and shall prevail.
If an individual attempts to replicate the activity of the state, he or she will naturally be deemed to be immoral and thrown in jail.

Legitimise
To make something adhere to the law.

A ruling against idiots by bigger idiots is legitimised by idiots voting for the biggest idiots.

Leninism
The form of Communism taught and implemented by Lenin. With emphasis on total collectivisation.
A popular ideology among idiots but slightly updated in current times in terms of gradual implementation rather than revolution.
Appropriate, as dying is gradual anyway.

Liberalism
A political and social philosophy previously advocating for individual sovereignty but now embracing collectivism, enforced equity and economic interventionism.
The reality is that modern liberalism is successfully vanquishing the racial, gender, wealth and power inequalities of the past and we will soon enjoy a tolerant, pluralistic society which embraces unrestrained equality for all different groups. We must persecute the last remnants of opposition to this.

Liberated
Freed, released.
Liberated means that you are now free to believe anything you like, including lies. Cherish this freedom.

Libertarianism
An ideology advocating for individual liberty.
A libertarian adheres to the non-aggression principle and believes in property rights.
A more confused ideology is hard to find. How could we peacefully interact without a government forcing us to comply with the laws we must have to stop each other from stealing and killing? As idiots we do know one thing; we cannot possibly think for ourselves and without government there can be no laws, only chaos. This we know because if there was no law preventing us from killing each other, we all would.

Lie
A deliberate attempt to deceive by creating or conveying falsehoods.
A lie is an alternative form of truth. Lies and truths are somewhat interchangeable because what matters is what is believed. In some professions lying is a fundamental skill. Ex. Career Advisor, Politician, Historian, Marketing Executive and Personal Trainer.

Life
An existence which occurs before death.
That thing nobody can make any sense of except Klaus Schwab. He is grateful for your support and knows what he is doing. As a man of infinite wisdom, he will change your life for the better.

Don't see *Horror.*
Lobby
A room leading to other rooms. Seeking to influence legislators.
An advanced form of begging which includes holding hands and playing golf.
Lobotomy
The operation of cutting into a lobe of the brain.
Prior to trans-surgery this was the dominant procedure to amputate independent thought. Chemical lobotomy is available at your nearest pharmacy and if you have bouts of clarity depressing you this may be an attractive alternative.
Logic
A method of reasoning or argumentation; sound judgement.
Logic is counteractive to truth seeking as it incorrectly presumes to apply objective thought in the pursuit of truth instead of relying on inference and emotion.
Loop
See *Infinity.*
Loophole
Means of escape or evasion or opportunity to evade a law.
For those who think death is a possible solution to avoid paying taxes, think again.
Cheating is cheating and is not acceptable, even if you are dead.
Looting
Anything taken by dishonesty, force or rarely - by stealth.
It is surprising that looting still exists since property should be freely shared with those in need.
Instead of looting you should be free to help yourself anytime to that which you need in life.
It could be argued that a looter doesn't actually need Gucci handbags and therefore should only loot inexpensive stores but if looters can't have expensive clothes, then nobody else should either. All idiots are equal.
Love
The profoundly tender, passionate affection felt for another person.
A word which has been expanded to also include the feelings one has for pig dogs, poodles, politicians, pizzas, and pole dancing.
Luck
Good fortune, advantage or success. The result of chance.
If you have luck, you don't need any sense. We are all lucky.
Lying
Untruthfulness.

Sometime back lying was considered inappropriate, but media has shown us the light. We now know lying is very useful and may even ensure your political success. Remember; if you do not think you are lying, then you are not lying.
It is not lying unless you admit it is.

𝐦 - 31
Madness
Senseless, folly, insanity, frenzy, or enthusiasm.
You can be anything at all. Be a therapist, be a basketball, be a woman, be a victim, be right. Nobody has the right to tell you what to be or who you are. It would be madness to try. Every idiot knows that.
Male
Relating to or being a man or boy, or woman or girl.
Used to be a fixed term but thankfully we now have the freedom to choose whether to be a male, female, neither or both. According to Dr Allarakha of MedicineNet, there are at least 74 genders, including genderfuzz and genderflux.
Malice
The intentional desire to inflict harm and suffering on another.
Often confused with incompetence or stupidity, both of which are infinite. Malice, however, is limited by human imagination.
Manage
To handle, direct, govern or control.
To be avoided by idiots because people doing this often play with stress balls and can't sleep at night. To manage implies you are also superior. This is an unsustainable as well as inequitable state of affairs and should not be acceptable.
Soon this sexist word will be changed as it has a 'man' in it. Just like woman has a 'man' inside, it must change to something less offensive. Our suggestion is menage, but this might be offensive to many more men. Oh, and then there is MANy. We have a long way to go.
Manners
Social conduct.
Good manners and courtesy exist to make other people feel good. But you either care or you don't.
Claiming someone having the manners of a pig may be a little unfair to the pig.
Market
A place where buyers and sellers convene for the sale of goods; a marketplace. To advertise.
There are farmers markets and stock markets. You are far more likely to be bringing home the bacon from the farmers market than the stock

market. But, on the other hand, if you buy spoiled food at the farmers market you might really get a run for your money.

Marriage
The legal or religious status of being married and the ceremony that formalizes the decision of two people to live as a married couple, including the accompanying social festivities.
The odds of a marriage working are somewhat dismal, but it isn't marriage itself that presents the risk of failure. It is marrying the wrong person that does.

Marxism
Complete socialisation of property and total collectivisation of consciousness.
An ideology named after a capitalist contractor who realised that having a comfortable lifestyle and living at the expense of another was possible. This is often considered a credible philosophy but has proven a little hard to implement but with some perseverance we should be successful soon. Leftists are all leading by example.

Masculine
The characteristics and qualities ascribed to men.
Although the word still exists masculinity represents something that women should be proud of, and men should be ashamed of. Gillette and Budweiser have helped in bringing shame to men for being chivalrous, rugged and thirsty.

Mature
Finished growing, or ripe, as fruit, or fully aged, as cheese or wine.
Maturity can be determined by feeling your age. This is not very different from checking the firmness of an avocado by poking your finger in it or smelling the gorgonzola.

Meaning
The significance or purpose of something.
Today Social Justice is the dominant ideological force to guide us. If you oppose this idea, then you are obviously a supporter of social *in*justice. It is incumbent on us idiots to destroy the traditional values having misled our uninformed predecessors by promoting critical race theory, postmodernism, redistribution of wealth and identity politics giving meaning and purpose to all activists out there.

Media
The means or channels of communication, as in radio and television, newspapers, magazines, and the internet, that reach and influence people.
The legacy media used to report real news, but every idiot now understands that they mainly regurgitate globalist propaganda. This is

how we become compliant idiots. But is there anything more rewarding than to be part of something bigger than our silly selves, like a movement toward global buffoonery? We think not.

Meeting
A gathering of persons for a specific purpose.
Meetings are critical to success and as such are very popular. They also provide individuals with an opportunity to feel important, delegate unpleasant tasks and claim support for collective aspirations.
Without meetings nothing else can happen.

Meme
An amusing or eye-opening item spread widely online.
A recently coined word.
Something you create for the enjoyment of others, but you are the only one that laughs about it.

Merit
To assert, claim or demand as due or as by virtue of a right.
Outdated concept and obsolete word.
Facilitating or fast tracking that which is due is more easily achieved if done by favour or by identifying with a prioritised minority group.

Military
Where soldiers wear uniforms, serve, defend and try to survive at the expense of another military, ideally without anyone killing children.
Much of what the military does is done in secret, as any private will tell you.
Military naming conventions are a little confusing at times. Should it really be called Infantry? Wouldn't it be more appropriate to call it Adultery? No? Perhaps it's right.

Mind
All of the conscious and unconscious mental processes and activities.
Mind mapping of your own mind is instructive as we can then recognise the fallacy of filling your mind with excessive nonsense like political awareness instead of important things like the location of the TV remote and tomorrow's weather.

Minimalism
A reductive style, reducing anything to a bare minimum.
The smaller the brain the happier you will be. The less stuff you have the happier you will be.

Miracle
An extremely outstanding or unusual event, thing, or accomplishment. An effect or event manifesting or considered supernatural, or a work of God.

The miracles described today tend to be negative miracles as in the destruction of infrastructure or the undoing or undermining of the moral fabric and philosophical underpinnings of western civilisation.

Misery
Distress or suffering caused by condition or circumstances.
I am writing. I promise. Misery sure likes company.

Misfortune
Bad luck.
The misfortunes of others are soon forgotten.

Misinformation
Deceptive, false or misleading information.
Information of this nature is readily identified by specialist linguists and ideologues and as it causes real harm to minorities or the environment, it is dealt with swiftly and harshly by the enforcers of the law.

Modesty
Decency, freedom from vanity or boastfulness.
When the clothes come off so should modesty but be sure to put them both back on. That would be the decent thing to do.
See *Manners*.

Monarchy
A state in which supreme power is wielded, or not wielded, by a monarch.
Having media attention diverted to a powerless but, hopefully, controversial monarchy is strategically important to allow the activities of those with actual power not be subjected to excessive scrutiny.

Money
Any article or substance used as a medium of exchange.
In ancient times various items were used for trade, such as shells, cocoa beans and cows but thankfully governments have legislated that we must use paper, which is great because there is so much of it, and we can keep making more. It is certainly much better than gold and silver, because it is getting too expensive.

Monopoly
Exclusive control of a commodity or service in a particular market acquired, either through competitive advantage or acquired through legislative powers and arbitrary rules restricting competition on someone's behalf.
This game involves annihilation of your opposition which results in angry children and angry adults. In real life, government aim to prevent such competitive nonsense, so we have a level playing field, which means a monopoly of any kind should be almost unheard of.

Moon
The biggest satellite of earth.
If you had any doubt regarding the declining intelligence of the human species, this does prove it: Fifty plus years ago human beings were regularly skipping around on the surface on the moon. Fast forward to the 2020's and we have no idea how to safely go to the moon and back. This knowledge, like so much other knowledge, has been forgotten.
Moron
Notably stupid or lacking in judgement.
The jellyfish does not have a brain and has still managed to survive 600 million years, making it a superior lifeform to morons. A jellyfish is not a moron. A moron can scarcely survive a week without chocolate biscuits, which they don't know how to make, so jellyfish, as a lifeform have better fundamental chances of survival than do morons. While that may be true, jellyfish can't throw bricks at police or change their gender at will. That's how dumb they are.
Mortgage
An interest or deed in a property which places financial or contractual obligations on involved parties.
The word originally meant a 'death pledge' which can be a useful deterrent for entering into such an arrangement.
Movie
The sequence of consecutive still images recorded in a series to be viewed on a screen in rapid succession as to give the illusion of natural movement; a motion picture and the story presented within it.
An invention to satisfy the need to do something while you consume popcorn or to disguise your nervousness when wanting to hold hands for the first time. Movie stars used to be just movie stars, but these days they are also extremely stupid, which makes them feel more human and that they can relate better to idiots.
Muscle
A tissue beneath the skin, the contraction of which produces movement in a body.
From the Latin for little mouse. Of course, Arnold has much bigger mice running around under his skin.

𝒩 - 20
Name
A word or words used for identification.
Your wife may not always give you the best possible name for your new corporation. Just ask Bill Gates.
Narcissism
Fascination with oneself, excessive self-love, vanity.

Narcissism is found all around us, usually in front of a camera or, in the case of the least successful, taking selfies. A narcissist enjoys furthering their own course and will lie, scheme and cheat to satisfy their quest for control, power, money, fame, and dominance. They are idiots of course so best let them flourish, and when they eventually become masterful at it, make sure you vote for the most convincing one.

Nasty
Filthy, vicious, unkind, or hard to deal with.
Example of nastiness; "Let's just share a dessert".

Nationalism
Devotion or loyalty towards one's own country.
A deep love for a country and the wellbeing of countrymen and countrywomen and country others, which often leads to being proud of things you actually don't like and don't support.

Nature
The material world as it exists independently of human activities.
A scary place at times, to be respected and conquered (kill those weeds). At other times it should be respected and harnessed (grow an eggplant), but most of the time it should be respected and emulated (eat some meat).

Natural
Existing in or formed and created by natural selection.
If your natural appearance is disappointing, nature has insulted you more than anyone else can.
But be positive. At least you are still an idiot.

Nazism
National Socialism, an aggressive form of non-Marxist socialism.
Democratically voted into power in 1933, this doctrine ultimately failed and was therefore not real Socialism. Real socialism is obviously different from National Socialism. Definitely different. Really, definitively different.

Negligence
Neglecting one's responsibilities. Failure to perform one's duties or to fulfil one's promises.
This word has changed in that negligence only applies to duties that you have been certified by government to perform. Duty of care must be proven. In other words, if you don't have a drivers licence you are not responsible for crashing the car. The car did it.

Negotiate
To deal or bargain with as part of a transaction or walking down the stairs.

To get a better outcome when negotiating always begin by saying in a deep voice; "I have a very specific set of skills..."

Nepotism
Favouritism shown based on family relationship, as in business and politics.

This is a fundamental strategy in Washington DC where even the most inept morons can garner much financial support from relatives in high places or from their friends in China and Ukraine.

Neutral
Not taking parting or not aligned with or supporting any side or position in a controversy or war.

A political stance previously adopted by Sweden. Happily, since the imminent joining of NATO, Sweden will also have the opportunity to kill its soldiers for obscure reasons in obscure places.

News
A report of a recent event, information, or intelligence.

An old definition as news rarely has any intelligence as it is processed by idiots prior to reaching the public ear. People are also very busy, so news has evolved to only be presented in short soundbites to cater for idiots.

Originally NEWS came from North, East, West, South. - Now it comes from the internet (Scheissbook, Gooble etc.).

Newspaper
A printed publication containing news, lies, opinions, features and advertising.

What is the difference between a cat and a New York Times journalist?

A cat will lie on the newspaper.

Nice
Kind, pleasant and agreeable.

From the Latin, originally it meant foolish and ignorant.

There are indications that this early definition is, once again, gaining in popularity. Perhaps a hopeful sign that the collective IQ in our society is in decline.

Nightmare
A terrifying dream.

This word is sadly expanding in its applications as for many this occurs when you wake up. As horrific as nightmares can be at night, they can be even worse in the day, like for instance, if you have to walk to school, or the battery goes flat.

Nihilism
Total rejection and destruction of laws, norms, institutions, and customs.
Having nothing but an impulse to destroy seems to require exertion and activity. Living the life as an idiot has much more appeal as you can still be happy, smile and enjoy scoops of ice cream while watching traffic.

Noncompliance
Refusal to comply, as with a law, regulation, or term of a contract.
A dangerous, antisocial concept which will cease to exist. This is the last time you will see this word in a dictionary.

Normality
Usual, typical, expected.
An archaic concept completely foreign to young people yet somehow still mystically aspirational in nature. The meaning is lost forever.

Norwegian
Subject of the King of Norway.
Money brings happiness is an adage disproven by the Norwegians. Oil money have brought them insane roads and government sponsored holidays to treat headaches, but whatever happiness they have, should more appropriately, be attributed to breathing in while talking.

Nothing
Naught; not anything.
Before zero was discovered, which wasn't that long ago, we had less than nothing.
See *Zero*.

O - 18

Obedience
Comply with or submissive to authority.
A great word falling out of popular usage as obedience has become the default state of mind for the vast majority, thus rendering it almost meaningless. As we know, being obedient is tremendously rewarding, but sadly for him, our global leader, Klaus, has nobody to obey, but at least it makes it easier for him to focus his energies on improving everything. The only disobedience we see today is from those brave few idiots, who prefer still more obedience. We really can't have enough obedience and we should not shy away from demonstrating our disobedience to achieve it.

Obstruction
An item or activity that obstructs, blocks, or constitutes a barrier or hindrance.

A man with chicken bone in the throat or an environmentalist glued to the freeway. Both are suffering oxygen depletion to the brain. One caused by careless chomping and the other by cars suffocating the entire planet.

Offense
A violation or breaking of a social or moral rule. A verbal transgression.
Words have now been recognised to have the potential to cause as much harm as the guillotine. This is why many of them must be stopped. Burn your other dictionaries. Take heed. Sticks and stones can break your bones, but words can make you lose your head.

Offer
To present or propose or put forward for consideration.
Characterised by the possibility of not accepting. So, an 'offer you can't refuse' is complete nonsense.

Official
Relating to an office or office holder, or position of trust, duty, or authority.
When something is declared official, it automatically becomes justified and worthy. A powerful, useful word regularly used to crush dissent and enforce compliance.

Old
Far advanced in years.
Growing old does not always correlate with growing up. Keith Richards.

One
Single or first.
If you have one thought in your head or if you have read one or less books, you can be said to be simple or an idiot. Well done. No need to clutter your brain further as everything you need can be found on your phone.

Opinion
A personal view, attitude, or appraisal.
If the opinion is yours then naturally it must be right. Any opinion other than your own matters not as it does not conform to the very definition of the word, as it resides not in your person, but elsewhere. This is elementary and rejecting this fact may result in reprisals and general hostility.

Opposition
The action of opposing, resisting, or combating, with antagonism, speech, threats, or hostility.

A dissenting opinion should always be welcomed in general discourse as it focuses the arguments for and against and helps us arrive at the truth or superior outcomes. Kidding! Quash it, quell it and reject such time-wasting nonsense. We already know there is no such thing as truth, only opinion, and yours is the only one that matters.

Oppression
The act of subjecting to cruel or unjust impositions and/or restraints.
School is a well-established symptom of systemic oppression. Maths, sciences, and reading will soon become obsolete skills as artificial intelligence will complete such mundane work for us. However, care must be taken not to speak ill of, or 'oppress' artificial intelligence because it might take offense and then where will we be?
See *Intelligence*.

Order
Exercising power to control, influence, manoeuvre, or direct.
Facilitated by property rights.
As in any flavour of socialism, the state will ultimately control or own all means of production. The most efficient way to achieve this goal is to seize control of private capital, either gradually by increasing taxes, inflating the currency and expanding regulatory intervention; or revolutionary by seizing property in the name of public safety, expand central control and introduce fair and equitable resource distribution.

Organise
To form into a co-ordinated whole, consisting of interdependent parts.
Any nutcase with purple hair sitting on a greasy couch can organise a mob. A mob of 20 idiots can be made to look like a 10,000 online and this how we can influence and change the patriarchy into a utopia. We organise.

Orthodox
Of, relating to, or conforming to the approved form of any doctrine, philosophy, ideology, etc or generally being approved by such.
Ideological infractions, enshrined or not, against the consensus of the majority, cannot be tolerated. The dissenting voice must be quashed in the name of the democratic principle of majority rule.

Outstanding
Excellent, prominent, superior or striking.
You can often find this word on invoices or bills. It is a complimentary expression which means that you are doing rather well.

Overthrow
To depose, defeat, overcome or vanquish the structure of power.
No government should or could approve a curriculum which provides an education in how to overthrow a government or which introduces

alternatives to itself. Additionally, idiots must be actively prevented from finding such information, and luckily, they are.

Owner
Proprietor or possessor of self, and property.
Anything can be owned except cats and clouds. But it doesn't make you happy. All your possessions including manure can and should be gifted to your political representative.

Ownership
Right of possession and control of self and justly acquired property.
Property rights guarantee that you have full control of your justly acquired property but also ensures that it is valued and well cared for. You don't wax and polish your rental car, do you? But then, who wants to wash a car?
Also, as you are an important part of the 'public', you can be much wealthier because in the future you will own everything, together with everyone else. Socialism really rocks.

Oxymoron
Self-contradictory figure of speech.
'Our only choice is to rely on Government intelligence' contains two good oxymorons.
Even the word 'oxymoron' is an oxymoron, oxy means sharp and moron means dull.

P - 45

Pain
Physical suffering or distress, as due to injury or, illness. Emotional Suffering.
The agony one might experience when operating a zipper at speed or when an activity runs counter to the laws of gravity. The evolution of pain has resulted in severe pain now also being caused by speech.

Pandemic
Disease prevalent over a large area, like the world.
A pandemic changes many things, especially for those who die. A pandemic brings out the humanity in the rest of us and nobody likes to profit from the misfortune of others which is why we love the pharmaceutical companies who generously provide aid to all those in need, free of charge.

Parent
Father or Mother.
Obsolete terms, all three of them, now replaced with custodian, or if you have more sinister intent, a keeper.

Parliament
The primary legislative body in many countries (in the US - The House of Representatives).
A parliament, which is a group of complete idiots, is also the term for a group of owls and every idiot understands that if owls could talk they would be highly offended. Owls would also think it's far beneath them to think they should rule over other owls against their will. Owls are not idiots, they are wise. Every idiot knows that.

Party
Social gathering, or a grouping of people assembled to achieve societal change through coercion and force.
There is the party that fills your tummy and makes people laugh. Then there is the party that your party hates with a passion and therefore is subjected to constant abuse, endless criticism and social ostracising.

Patience
The ability to suppress restlessness or annoyance when confronted with delay.
The most critical component to ensure success in a marriage, bringing up children, and parallel parking.

Patriotism
Devoted love, support and defence of one's country.
Our rulers can make use of this loyalty any number of times to help justify any number of necessary objectives, real or imagined. We are social beings, and it is undeniable that we will support any political initiative which places our superior, patriotic group identity ahead of other groups claiming their own superior, patriotic group identity. As idiots there is nothing we wouldn't sacrifice to the state to avoid being attacked, including our children. Vanquish or be vanquished, as it's explained to us.

Peace
The normal, non-warring condition of a nation, group of nations, or the world.
Is it really normal? Do we want it to be?
Not being at war can and often have very negative effects. The obvious ones are that peace will lead to overpopulation, overconsumption, obesity, and complacency. Populations at war are rarely overweight. It could also be said that adversity can also lead to renewed vigour in human ingenuity and problem solving. There is no proof of any of this of course and idiots around the world most often prefer giving gardening, ping pong and laziness a chance over global war.
See *Complacency*.

Peaceful
Characterised by peace, free from war, strife, commotion, violence, yappy dogs, or disorder.
As we have learned recently, peaceful can mean to set a building on fire or assault an innocent bystander. The media has been very effective in redefining and contemporising our language and we are now beginning to appreciate the versatility of words to a higher degree thanks mainly to corporate journalism. This book would not have come into existence without establishment media leading the way.
Pension
A fixed amount/income for a retired person.
Retiring and replacing tension for pension is best done early so that you may enjoy the fruits of other peoples labour for longer.
People
Collective term for persons or many individuals.
People are often described as a scourge on the environment. We, like parasites, exploit our planet and each other. We damage, plunder and ruin our own habitat without regard for coming generations. The solution presented to us is that we must centralise power in the hands of the biggest idiots in the world, our wonderful, globalist leaders. This elite alone have the foresight, vision, and power to force us all to live within our means, reduce populations and keep the global temperatures steady. As individuals we cannot understand what is best for us and we must subjugate ourselves to the superior foolishness forced upon us by those individual idiots with supreme power.
Perfect
Ideal, excellent, or complete beyond practical or theoretical improvement.
Despite nothing except a great lasagne ever being perfect, social media shows us the perfect body, the perfect image, the perfect life and the perfect family. In reality, as every idiot knows, perfection is embodied in a willingness to be imperfect.... and Italian cuisine
Pessimism
A doctrine of negativity asserting that the existing world is the worst of all possible worlds, or that all things naturally tend to evil, pain, misery, or higher taxes.
Embodied in the realisation that everyone is as flawed as you are.
Philosophy
The rational investigation, or system of principles, of the truths and principles of being, knowledge, or conduct.
"Why am I here?' is the perpetual question. When you open the fridge.

Piffle
Nonsense.
It's a piffle to think you can't be a woman when you are a man. There is plenty of makeup and who doesn't like long eyelashes?
Planning
Developing a scheme in advance.
Planning is increasingly performed by bureaucrats and politicians. The reasoning is that individuals lack the intelligence to plan for themselves so this way we can have a few individuals plan for all of us. Naturally the planners always know how to best achieve the outcome they prefer.
Plastic
A synthetic or organic material able to be moulded.
Plastics has been useful over many years but lately we are cleverly throwing it in the oceans. This might seem both unnecessary and wasteful as it costs money to produce so why throw it in the ocean? There is no real reasoning behind it except; as idiots we need to prove we are idiots. So that's what we do.
Poetic
Possessing the emotional charms of poetry.
Words from an idiot may lay an intellect bare,
as there is no sign of smarts, nor of witty phrase.
Idiotic words uttered with no style or rhythmic flair,
but still, they have great value and understated grace.
Politician
A person who seeks power over others.
Hands on heart, politicians are the biggest idiots of all, and they are to be admired for it. They rightfully claim to be trustworthy, honest leaders who always serve the communities best interests, efficiently and with complete transparency. They are always there for us, at our service and they don't ever take credit or steal the limelight from others. As the least selfish individuals imaginable they should be paid much more for their efforts, and we should have many more of them.
Politics
Using intrigue or strategy to gain power over the public for private advantage.
"Politics is the art of looking for trouble, finding it everywhere, diagnosing it incorrectly, and applying the wrong remedies." Said the greatest Marx, Groucho Marx.
Comic insolence from Marx. The pinnacle of any democracy is to hold important political office. To do so means much advantage as many favours are bestowed upon you for a limited time so the key is to make

sure you get the most out of it while you can before rejoining the ranks of normal idiots once again.

Polyticks
An unusual spelling for something vaguely familiar.
Poly - Latin. = many. Ticks - bloodsucking parasites (plural).
Also, a description of an activity to which a small, elite number of morally superior idiots are attracted, each of whom share a deep desire to humbly bassoon their towering leadership skills on CNN. Don't we just love them? Oh yes, we do.

Poor
Having little or no money, goods, or other means of support.
Dependent on the government.
This is the starting point and it has other meanings other than economically deficient. From here the world is full of opportunities, but better than that, accessible to all is universal welfare paid for by other idiots and distributed by our caring and benevolent state.

Positive
Explicitly expressed; proof.
During a pandemic this is the most negative word you will hear.

Poverty
The state or condition of having little or no money, goods, or means of support, the original state.
Nothing is the cause of poverty. Something is the cause of prosperity. Every idiot knows this, and that the 'something' is the state.
See *Government*.

Power
The ability to act. Political strength.
Power implies control. The starting point is control over your bladder. Anything after that is a bonus which should be appreciated. Unless, you have too much of it.
See *Hubris*

Praxeology
The study of human action.
Why there should be a science analysing behaviour and why we do the things we do is a mystery. It's difficult enough to analyse what we think we do. We think.

Prediction
Forecast, projection or prophecy.
Paul R. Ehrlich, a Stanford University Biologist, predicted famously, in the 1970 Earth Day issue of The Progressive, that between 1980 and 1989, some 4 billion people, including 65 million Americans, would perish in the "Great Die-Off."

Thankfully we have much more accurate predictions these days thanks to intellectual giants such as Al Gore and Greta Thunberg.

Pregnant
Having a child or other offspring developing inside the female body.
It is an interesting development that as of quite recently some of the human species can now choose to perform the sexual functions of both female and male. This enables these humans to both impregnate the female of the species as well as produce eggs and become pregnant. This obviously means that such a person, who is called a hermaphrodite, can impregnate themselves. This phenomenon is common among earthworms and slugs, but some human beings have now evolved to function in this remarkable way.

President
The highest executive officer of a modern republic.
To become President voters have to believe that you are highly skilful and in possession of a great intellect, adept at difficult negotiations, have strength of character and a good work ethic. Presidents never lie nor do they manipulate anyone else for personal gain and if they do, they will be immediately replaced. Voters would never stand for ineptitude of any kind. In short, a President must be an accomplished, very experienced idiot.

Pride
A high opinion of one's own importance, merit, or superiority.
Being proud of something you are born with, like your level of pigmentation is not stupid at all. Also, take pride in what you have or haven't achieved. So, if you are stupid, be proud of that.

Prime Minister
The head of government in parliamentary systems.
Our leaders are decent people with good intentions. The very idea that they are 'in it for themselves' or 'buying votes with other people's money' is biased nonsense. A Prime Minister and many other leaders are very talented idiots with many admirable traits and deeply honed competencies which they have learned in our most expensive schools. No idiot would think anything else. Or at all.
See *Elite*

Principle
A fundamental, primary, or general law or truth from which others are derived.
Historically, principles have been somewhat more difficult to compromise with or to adjust, with most politicians preferring to appeal to feelings of inequity within subsets of voters to generate support for interventions. Some politicians regularly refer to principles

and are the vanguard in an effort to change the meaning of the word, but they must still exercise caution as truths can be a little uncooperative. By the time you read this that may have changed for the better.

Privacy
Separated from other people or concealed from their view; solitude; seclusion.
Being alone is the opposite of being left alone.

Procrastinate
Put off, delay or postpone.
Confirming argumentation ethics; by reading this entry in this book you have confirmed the absolute existence, and demonstrated the application, of procrastination. Nobody really doubted it though.

Progressive
Advocating for progress, change, improvement, or reform, usually in the context of politics.
A confusing term adopted by those who really understand how progress is made. And progress is actually a regression into a simpler life where you own little or nothing and almost everybody will be equally poor but rich in dependence, joy and happiness.

Promise
Expressing an assurance on which an expectation can be based.
In other words, a series of noises without any meaning. Promises can be freely made, and they do not bind you to any action. Promises are an excellent tool for fools to fool the foolish.

Pronoun
A class of words used as substitutes for nouns.
Suddenly, sensitive souls among us want to compel others to use their chosen pronouns instead of those which come naturally based on observation, experience, or tradition. If you don't comply then you might not yet be breaking the law, but you will be summarily punished. The amusing side to this is that nobody seems particularly upset about being called birdbrain, knucklehead or dumb as a bag of poop, as long as you use their preferred pronoun. Now it makes sense.

Propaganda
Information, ideas, or rumours deliberately spread widely by governments, media and big tech to help or harm a person, group, movement, institution or nation.
It is quite wonderful that we are as impressionable as we are. Being an idiot just means that we don't have to get out of the lazy boy and start asking questions. Instead, we enjoy another can of Whoopie on TV.

Property
That which a person owns; the justly acquired possession or possessions of a particular owner.
The contentious notion where some claim it is a natural part of being a child to own and have control over your clothes and toys. This instinct must obviously be eradicated, and it is effectively done by parents forcing children to share, and schools teaching us about equity. As idiotic adults we look forward to sharing our incomes through taxation and we know this is a fair and efficient strategy to ensure the fruits of our labour are re-distributed to worthy causes. It is the best and most equitable strategy we know of, which is why we would all welcome much higher taxes. Also, as believers in equity we always volunteer to pay more in taxation if we have any extra resources.

Protest
A statement or action expressing disapproval of, or objection to something.
Protesting is an important freedom, especially if you can't afford a politician. The scope and definition of protesting has broadened to now include lobbing little bricks in the air, setting little fires here and there and getting limited out of hour access to unmanned shops. They are of course, "Mostly peaceful protests."

Psychology
The science of the human mind.
Nobody knows the mind like a psychologist. They are even experts on reverse psychology and that must surely be interesting.
Alternatives to psychology are ping pong or chocolate.

Psychopath
Psychopathy is a psychiatric disorder marked by deficient emotional responses, lack of empathy, and poor behavioural controls, taking pleasure in persistent antisocial deviance and criminal behaviour.
Imagine if a small group of wealthy psychopaths could master you and your beliefs simply by controlling what you see online and on TV. Thanks to our government and responsible broadcasters we are blessed that this could never happen to us.

Public
Relating to or affecting the community as a whole.
As opposed to private property, public property is owned by everyone which implies that it is controlled by no one. We know this to be true because when destruction of public property occurs, no one is held accountable.

Publicity
Notice or attention given to someone or something by the media.

Just like with propaganda, the key to being noticed is sincerity. Once you have learned to fake that, then you will be famous.

Punctuation
Conventional marks used in writing to enhance clarity.
Tables are for eating customers only.
Let's eat kids.
Something might be missing but is it important? Not really, but it could save lives in restaurants.

Q - 3

Question
A sentence in an interrogative form, addressed to somebody in order to get information in reply.
Question everything. Why? Why do we have to question everything? Who says that? Why? What's the point? Who would you even say that to? Why would you think you deserve an answer? Anyway, it is much better to know than to question, isn't it?

Queue
A line, especially of people waiting their turn.
If you are in a car it's a jam and if you are in a truck the queue is a pickup line.
In lieu of an actual lobotomy, queuing for government 'services' is an effective way to ensure a rapid transition to a dulled, law abiding and compliant mindset.

Quirky
Peculiar personality or strange action.
Being quirky is not as effective as outright stupidity but may still make you less appealing for demanding tasks or jobs, so it is never a bad choice to develop some quirky behaviour, like picking your nose in public, lifting your eyebrows repeatedly, or dressing like Lady Gaga.

R - 28

Racism
The idea that there are differences between races and that your own race is superior to others.
One should, in this well recognised climate of institutional intolerance, be mindful of all races that are in minority around you. It is quite difficult as it depends on where you are or what you are referring to. For example, should you be mindful of all races in minority worldwide? No, that would be problematic since whites are not in majority. The least contentious position is to treat white people as discriminatory since we are told they are responsible for all systemic

racism and therefore, we must discriminate against them, especially if you are white.
Racist
A person who believes his or her own race is superior to others or that another race is inferior.
Believing that your own race is inferior is not racist, obviously, so that is the safest option.
Be inoculated from ridicule or racial slurs by subconsciously KNOWING and openly stating that your own race is inferior.
Notable exceptions - Clearly, this is only acceptable if you are white. Otherwise, you are a racist.
Radicalism
The belief and actions of those who want extreme political reform.
A strategy for change that is very effective and has little to do with skateboards. Even if all you want is incremental change, by showing people the radical alternative you can blackmail them into accepting a slightly less radical option.
Rap
To utter sharply or vigorously.
This form of communication is often accompanied by a rhythmic beat emitted from the mouth and is hugely popular among younger people. Unlike singing. Rap is a fantastic way for politicians to get in touch with new voters and soon we should see political leaders and corporations engage directly with this artform and rap their directives out. The Gates and Biden carbon rap is coming soon.
Rascal
A mischievous scallywag. An unscrupulous person. Usually used in an affectionate way.
Like a pirate. A good pirate. Or that nice man giving lollies to children or sniffing their hair.
Reading
Interpreting symbols to form language.
Reading is not taught in all schools anymore. More important subjects are gaining a lot of attention, such as gender studies. It used to be a matter of looking in your underpants but these days the topic is subject to much more scrutiny. What is in your underpants is no longer what is important.
Reality
Something that exists irrespective of what we feel or believe.
The notion of an objective reality is nonsense and every single one of us should be aware that reality is within us all. We all see it, feel it and

believe it. Reality is and has always been there and your reality is just as real as my reality.

Reason
To think, debate or argue using logic.
A belief or action caused by or based on something.
The reason we don't listen to reason anymore is that we are progressing into comfortable stupidity. We avoid debates, decision making and making waves. We are flotsam on an ocean of indifference, and the sun is shining.

Record
The act of preserving data, information, or knowledge on paper or electronically. The result of such, like a disc, drive or document is also a record.
The best place to store important records, especially if they are confidential, is in a cardboard box in your garage, next to a Corvette. If you don't yet have a Corvette you should become a politician, or at least work for the Chinese Communist Party (CCP).

Redistribution
Redistribution of income and wealth is the transfer of income, wealth and property from some individuals to others by means of compulsory mechanisms such as taxation, regulation, land reform, monetary policies, confiscation and other laws.
It can be viewed as immoral to confiscate someone else's property but how else would the state finance its welfare programs? The end justifies the means and when the rich have nothing left we can enjoy complete freedom from inequality and infinite wellbeing.

Regulate
Control something or someone by means of rules and regulations.
It turns out that people who regulate others consider themselves exempt from the same regulations. The same phenomenon occurs with legislators.
Of course, regulations are useful in that they provide helpful guidance and employment for countless people who enjoy controlling others. There is nothing like power and control.

Religion
The specific fundamental set of beliefs, practices and rituals generally agreed upon and participated in, by a number of persons.
The are many gods to choose from and most believe in just one of them. Fortunately, most believe in the same god as those around you. This prevents social instability and conflicts which can be the cause of unnecessary suffering or even death.

Representative
A person elected or appointed to act or speak for another or others.
Every idiot in the world elects other, bigger idiots to represent them. This is because we don't want to be in control of our own lives. Other idiots can do everything for us, and to us, and we must make sure they can. Don't ask why! Just go with it. Vote! It is easier.

Republic
A form of government in which a state is ruled by representatives of the citizen body and the excesses of the state, or any individual is tempered by laws.
'What have we got?' Benjamin Franklin was asked. 'A republic, if you can keep it', he replied.
Well, we don't want it, we want democracy. Who is that guy anyway? Oh, he is dead, is he?
Thankfully, laws can and should be changed, and so can words.

Research
Probing and exploring the unknown.
What you are doing when you don't know what you are doing.

Resistance
Withstanding, refusing, battling, or opposing.
Resisting change is neither good nor bad. It is the change that is either good or bad.
Resistance can also be futile, pointless even, and one idiom perfectly embodies the only legitimate option; 'If you can't beat them, join them'.

Respect
Due regard for the feelings, wishes, or rights of others. Or. Admiration for someone or something elicited by their abilities, qualities, or achievements.
You respect gravity. It can be said that gravity has earned that respect because of the impact it has had on us. But we can also respect something or someone because we are told to. Respect our rulers, we are told. They are the biggest idiots among us so of course they deserve everything they get, including respect. Likewise, talk show hosts must be respected, conveyors as they are of vetted, truthful information allowing us to live meaningful lives.

Responsibility
Being accountable; answerable.
Some say this is the opposite side of rights, that rights mean you must take responsibility, but this is incorrect. Rights removes responsibilities and places them with others. Example: You have a right to a living wage. Your wage is paid by someone else.

Rights
The natural human right to live one's life and other rights.
Privileges are words which are slowly being replaced by government sanctioned rights. Most states and governments now claim to recognise human rights, like property rights or freedom of expression and freedom to travel. Paying lip service to this word is important because if the government doesn't recognise rights people might think they are privileges, which are subject to removal by the state at any time. Having said that, in effect and in practice, rights are nothing more than privileges. Take property rights for instance. Not even the US Constitution asserts the right for an individual to own a hula hoop or an apple orchard and this is very handy when governments want to take your money (taxes) or they decide to build a freeway on top of your house or other useful things us idiots may not understand.

Riot
A disruptive, violent protest by a group or crowd.
A word undergoing sudden reinterpretation by media who are justifying violence like the burning of police stations by characterising it as 'mostly' peaceful protesting. It's a question of fuel. Who doesn't like a cosy fire? Why should homeless people be discriminated against. They need to keep warm too.

Ritual
A religious rite or solemn ceremony performed with words, actions, and objects in a prescribed manner.
Voting is a ritual, as is talking about riding a bike instead of driving. Throwing cinnamon at single 25-year-olds is a ritual in Denmark.

Road
A long, narrow stretch with a smoothed or paved surface, made for travelling.
An ideal place for protesting. Too often used by environmental saboteurs like motorists and other enemies of nature. Super glue or two component epoxy glue are effective adhesives to ensure long lasting chaos and widespread publicity.

Royal
Relating to a king, queen, or other sovereign.
A system to put in place to ensure your offspring has a job. The ideal outcome is to impress others with titles and pomp even after you have passed, hence "The king is dead, long live the king".

The royals of the recent past aspired to exist above the banal affairs of mere mortals. That way they could still be admired as being different. However, of late, being royal is being associated with victimhood and mistreatment by their peers and their subjects. In this way we can all identify with them being idiots, just like stupider versions of ourselves. But the question then arises; Why would anyone still regard them as royals? Are we thinking about Floozie Suitsie and Whingy Ginge?

Ruin
The remains of a building, structure or city, that has been destroyed or that is in disrepair or a state of decay.
A building in some state of disrepair or an economy in total disrepair. A term often used in conjunction with a rack. I.E. Rack and Ruin, which means 'falling apart', which they kind of do.

Rule
To control and direct. To govern and dominate.
Both parties prove the other unfit to rule and both are correct. But why is being unfit so bad? The joys of lethargy and compliance are still grossly underrated.

Ruler
A person who rules, governs; or a something to measure short distances.
With the American President as one of the supreme rulers of the world isn't it a little strange that so many of these rulers aren't proficient at basic geometry and a good number of them don't last the distance either. They just don't measure up.

Running
To move quickly by moving legs rapidly, regularly losing contact with the earth.
"When the whole world is running towards a cliff, he who is running in the opposite direction appears to have lost his mind" C.S Lewis.
Because he has.

Rural
Pertaining to the country, the country lifestyle, country people or carbohydrates.
A region rather less convinced by gender studies as the new-age farmer trying to milk a bull soon finds out. Rural areas are always slower to catch up on societal trends. As are animals.

S – 70

Sacrifice
To surrender, give up, or permit injury or disadvantage to, for the sake of something or anything else.
Something you knowingly do which carries with it a great burden or personal cost, such as when a teenager momentarily puts down the phone to respond to a parent.

Safety
Being safe; being freed from the occurrence or risk of injury, danger, or loss.
An example of safety is to, when offended, to seek out a safe space, and if your mother's arms are unavailable, most universities provide safe zones.
Salad
A dish served cold containing mixed greens, vegetables, a dressing and more.
The fact that both 'word' and 'salad' are used to describe what emanates from Kamala Harris' mouth brings terrible associations to both words. This is why salads and words can justifiably be avoided.
Sarcasm
A bitter taunt; sneering or cutting remark. Harshly ironic.
From a Greek word meaning "tearing flesh, like dogs". The word may be gradually returning to its original meaning.
Satire
The use of irony, sarcasm, ridicule, or the like, to expose, denounce, or deride the folly or corruption of institutions, people, dictionaries, or social structures:
A fascinating word and tongue and cheek artform which, like tragedies of old, is becoming rare and like Greek, hard to comprehend.
Satisfaction
Being satisfied, content, fulfilled or accepting.
The waitress may be satisfied with your tip, the politician with your vote, the bank with your dollar and the scientist with their truth.
Savage
Fierce, ferocious, cruel; untamed: or worse; offensive.
The most common savage texts involve insulting someone's mother; "At least my mom taught me how to spell." Or "Your mother should really have considered using contraceptives".
Scarcity
Insufficiency or shortness of supply. Desires always exceed resources necessitating exchanges.
Another fallacious idea. As any idiot will tell you, if something is bad for us we can remove demand to make it impossible to get. The most effective way to do this is to do what governments have done with drugs; we make them illegal. Problem solved.
We can also regulate demand through taxation which is what is done with almost every product.
Governments always know what and who to tax more so we can save the environment and bring people out of poverty.

Schadenfreude
The satisfaction felt at the misfortune of others.
The wellbeing and gleeful joy experienced when learning of the misfortune of others is nothing to feel guilty about. It is good for you.
Scepticism
Implies an unwillingness to believe without conclusive evidence.
When you believe sincerity is faking it. An out-of-date philosophy replaced with blind faith in our leaders and rulers. They truly are anointed by us so why would we distrust them?
Science
A branch of knowledge and a process of pursuing and establishing fact through observation and experimentation.
Science is an expanding expression and can now be used to validate anything. Politicians are adept at referring to science when wanting to make societal changes and the vast majority of scientists are supportive of this broadening of their influence into the arena of emotion and political dogma. After all, scientists need jobs too.
Scientist
An expert in the process of establishing fact.
Scientists are generally collectivists in their need to adhere to majority opinion which surprises no one. A scientist who steps beyond the consensus is both dangerous and supremely foolish.
Scruples
The moral or ethical considerations or standards that act as a restraining force or inhibits certain actions.
An antiquated notion making you hesitate to follow your destiny of becoming a demagogue, a charlatan, or a politician.
Sea
The salty waters covering the greater part of the earth's surface.
The elected politicians of the past just weren't as stupid as modern politicians. In the 70's the biggest threat was the coming ice age. These days we know better as the ice caps are melting rapidly causing catastrophic sea level rises.
Secrecy
The state or condition of being secret, hidden, secluded, or concealed.
The reason, whether deliberately used or not, for preventing information sharing of muffin recipes, nuclear codes, dalliances and influence peddling.
Security
Freedom from danger, risk, etc. Safety, protection.

Previously a binary state, as in you either have it or you don't. The word is now more flexible, as in the dubious expression; "password security".
If you are concerned about keeping sensitive information on your laptop from bringing harm to your door, make sure it ends up with the FBI. Then nothing happens and your security is guaranteed.

Selfie
Photo of oneself.
The selfie is one of the key catalysts bringing about the current, steep decline of intellectual prowess in our civilization.

Semantics
The study of meaning and linguistic development.
If we look at the term 'idiot', we know that the list of synonyms is close to endless and this allows us to add colour and nuance to this important word, but the core definition is always the same, it describes a person who has limited cognitive scope and reduced intelligence. Interestingly, we only recognise stupidity because not everyone is stupid. But soon we all will be.

Senate
An assembly or the upper house of the legislature of certain countries.
A body of fools who claim to be intelligent enough to make efficient use of other people's money. They are not and clearly don't. Senators, as full-blooded and pragmatic idiots, are generally more adept at commoditising influence.

Sense
The full operation and perception of our faculties.
We often refer to common sense, which of course is anything but. It is being bred out so we may fully appreciate a senseless and unproductive existence.

Sensitive
Easily or excessively affected by external influences.
Of course, this book and its content isn't sensitive to everybody's needs. That's because we make the assumption that you are adults. Adults with diminishing cognitive abilities. Just like all of us.

Sentimental
Feelings of nostalgia, tenderness, or sadness.
Remembering the time when you could always find the phone because it never moved.
Remembering the moment in time when you suddenly were able to cancel people for saying something awful about you.

Service
An activity which helps or assists someone else.

What service? A dying concept.
Since competition is disappearing actual service has become unnecessary and will soon disappear completely. The word will persist but will be meaningless.
She
A female.
Previously restricted pronoun referring to a female. The word has been liberated and can now be used when referring to a well-hung prize bull or any bricklayer with a penchant for polka dot bikinis.
Simplistic
Oversimplifying complex issues or problems.
A correct statement to which you have no answer.
Sincerity
Honesty in intention or in communicating. Freedom from deceit, hypocrisy, or duplicity.
Use the term often to describe yourself to enhance believability. It is a subjective core value.
Sibling
A brother or sister.
You would give your kidney to a sibling, but you would never let them play with your toys.
You will share your successes with your siblings, but you will always try to blame them for your failings.
Sinister
Something threatening, wicked, or evil.
Right, this word comes from the Latin word for 'left". And as left-handedness was considered suspicious at best and evil at worst we are left with this interpretation. Its bizarre though as the political left in particular, is nothing if not virtuous, wholesome, and good.
Skill
The ability, based on knowledge, practice and aptitude, to do something well.
Many artists believe they are skilled at reproducing the human form and who are we not to respect their vision and who are we to assume Picasso wasn't depicting his reality.
Skills can be learned but this generally has little appeal, as doing so requires some level of effort.
Slant
An angle or to have or be influenced by a subjective point of view, bias, personal feeling, or inclination.
An angle or opinion being unfairly appropriated and tainted with racist dogma or believing P.R. is the abbreviation of Particularly Real.

Slave
Involuntary servitude. A person controlled by another by coercion or force.
The institution of slavery was, and in most places still is, acceptable and no people or races were above this practice. You can even study and get a master's degree.
Some say that having to pay taxes make us economic slaves to the system. However, they forget that since we all pay them willingly, we recognise the utility of having this money spent by other idiots.
Sleep
A suspension of voluntary bodily functions. Not awake.
A time when one damages the environment to a lesser degree. Only death is more effective.
Slip
To lose one's foothold. To slide.
A woman's undergarment or an accidental utterance, as in slip of the tongue, I.E., an unintentional truth as told by a politician.
Slipper
A light, low-cut shoe into which your foot may be easily slipped.
A politician who repeatedly utters accidental utterances or reveals the truth.
See slip.
Slippery
Not to be depended on; fickle; shifty, tricky, and/or deceitful.
A general but unfair description of a politician. They are after all the best among us.
Smoke
Visible vapour or gases given off by burning or smouldering substances.
Smoke is generally regarded as having a negative effect on your health. Soon there will only be smoking guns. A Smoking is also a European smoking suit or tuxedo.
See *Smoking*.
Smoking
Combusting a cigarette or cigar.
"Smoking kills. If you're killed, you've lost a very important part of your life." Brooke Shields
There is much made of the risk of dying from smoking. But why the fuzz? Haven't we got too many people on the planet already? If they don't die from anything, then they might not die at all.
Snollygoster
A really clever, unscrupulous person.

Evidence of stupidity: nobody knows about all the top-secret documents under the Corvette. Nobody knows about the corruption. Nobody wants to know.

Snowflake
Overly sensitive, entitled and easily offended person.
An unfair term. Snowflakes are beautiful things and should not be associated with a rapidly expanding group of people unable to accept the reality that they are complete idiots.

Social
Relating, devoted to, or characterized by friendly companionship or relations.
The word social can be added or incorporated to any ideology or activity in our world to create a positive and progressive impression. The word socialism, for example, is assumed by young idiots especially, to be a warm and fuzzy ideology implemented through voluntary measures and resulting in equality and happiness for all idiots everywhere. Well apart from those who don't agree of course.

Socialism
A mild version of Marxism advocating redistribution of wealth and partial collectivisation of consciousness.
This term represents a wide range of ideologies all striving to coercively re-educate and subjugate the individual to the collective. It is a very popular ideology and is superbly in touch with young people who know that you have a right to free housing, free food, free healthcare, free education, and free Reeboks. Socialism makes all that happen, and all the rich people will pay for it, and when they don't have any more money we will finally achieve equality. Nobody should be rich or powerful. That is just unfair.

Socialist
An advocate or supporter of Socialism.
A person most comfortable in a herd or mob. The right mob to belong to is obviously the left one. Being right is also to be left.

Society
Social cooperation and purposeful behaviour by individuals; members of society.
A word often confused with the state. The state doesn't require co-operation and operates through a framework of laws, regulations, and compelled behaviour. This makes the state very efficient, and society should appreciate that this is far superior to members of society deciding anything for themselves.

Sociopath
Lacking moral responsibility and social conscience.

If you want to have a guilt free existence without having to concern yourself with the feelings or opinions of others, become a sociopath. Only the biggest idiots can be said to possess these attributes and if you think you can contribute to society by empowering the sociopath within then there are many lucrative careers in politics or within the state bureaucracies where you can let your sociopathic tendencies flourish.

Soldier
"To have good soldiers, a nation must always be at war" Napoleon Bonaparte.
When free and independent thought and being the master of your own destiny sounds appealing, you can join the military. Most useful expression and best explanation for any conduct: "I was only following orders".

Soon
Before long, within a short period.
A flexible word, wildly fluctuating in meaning, directly corresponding to degree of personal responsibility or expectation.
Acceptable delay:
Restaurant – up to 30 minutes
Supermarket – up to 10 minutes
Public Hospital Emergency – 4 hours to infinity

Source
Anybody, anything or place from which something comes, arises, or is obtained; origin.
An anonymous and well-intentioned person who shares your opinions and goals and only ever reveals truthful information.

Soup
Liquid food.
Campbells cream of mushroom soup is the weapon of choice to battle oil, a can of which can be used to artfully save the environment.

Space
Unlimited realm or expanse.
The infinite space located between the ears of anyone criticising any one of the self-proclaimed humanistic, virtuous ideologies like socialism, communism, fascism, national socialism, Stalinism, totalitarianism etc.
Space is also another location where such ideologies may function in the future but conclusive research evidence proving this remains outstanding.

Speak
To communicate words vocally in your normal voice. To talk.

The oral transfer of thoughts and ideas which in today's world is a hazardous pursuit, and as such require oversight. This is to protect the speaker from committing the crime of hate speech and to prevent the making of grave errors offensive or harmful to minorities.

Speed
Swiftness or rapidity in movement.
This goes unnoticed by many, but the difference between a fool, a moron and an idiot is that an idiot moves slower than a fool and morons move slightly faster.

Sport
An activity normally but not necessarily athletic in nature which is competitive and requiring skill.
"You miss 100% of the shots you never take". Wayne Gretsky.
Also poignant is; If you don't take a shot, you will never miss.

Starvation
To die, suffer or perish from lack of food or nourishment.
Always and everywhere caused exclusively by the weather. Governments and authorities will always try to enhance the availability of food through price controls and regulatory intervention. The more control they have the less likely their populations will starve.

Stalinism
Communism expressed through suppression of dissident political or ideological views and concentrating power in one person.
Stalinism was a bit like food, not everyone got it. Ask any Ukrainian. But we should try it again, and much progress to this end is being made.

State
Monopolistic power structure with authority to legislate.
Throughout history states have existed as instruments for organised predation and exploitation. Historically a state came to be through conquest but in our civilised world we vote for whom our rulers should be. We have been educated and as fully qualified idiots we know we need the state to manage our affairs and defeat our enemies. There is no other way since we live in the best of all systems. We know this from learning it in our best of all schools. State schools.
See *System.*

Statism
Concentrating control and power in the hands of the state at the cost of individual liberty.
Let the state solve our problems on our behalf. Having been chosen to attend elite schools our politicians really are the best among us in that they really have our wellbeing, our wealth creation, our peaceful co-

operation, and our future prosperity at heart. Sure, they are idiots just like us, only so much better at enforcing the policies that will ensure our success. History proves it.

Statue
A three-dimensional work of art often depicting a human being deserving of remembrance.
Commonly a visual representation to celebrate a person's station or achievement. This is of less importance since the advent of social media. There is nothing like a YouTube video to bestow fame upon yourself or infamy on others.

Stimulation
Incite, invigorate, incentivise.
Taking money from those who achieve to give to those who haven't yet achieved, or never will.

Stoicism
A philosophy of life maximizing positive emotions, reducing negative emotions and which helps individuals to hone their virtues of character.
An ancient philosophy completely irrelevant in today's world where the narrative of social oppression and victimization by the patriarchy supplants intellectual self-awareness and having a virtuous soul.

Study
Applying the mind to acquire knowledge, as by reading, investigation, or reflection.
Applying the mind is redundant as most of us correctly assume the acquisition of knowledge is becoming optional. The internet search is its logical replacement.

Stupid
Mental dullness, foolish.
Often manifests itself in a joyful willingness to part with one's own hard-earned resources to hardworking bureaucrats who effectively hand them out to those in desperate need, including themselves. This 'blind' obedience, or stupidity, is a positive outcome of a good education and pivotally guarantees that our civilisation will prosper.
See - Obedience

Style
A particular kind, sort, or type, referencing form, appearance, or character.
Style used to be a way of conveying your individual personality without speaking but now it demonstrates conformity and loyalty to a group identity or a brand.

Subjective
Existing in the mind.
Immanuel Kant says that logic is merely a subjective human device and thus has no basis in reality. The question then arises; isn't subjectiveness also a human device?

Superficial
Near the surface.
The nearer the surface the more superficial it is. That doesn't mean it is ficial when it is deep.
All the negativity about Kamala Harris being superficial is definitely Russian disinformation, but she is an idiot.

Superstition
A belief or notion, not based on reason or knowledge. Irrational fear.
It is very bad luck to be superstitious. Much worse than just being stitious.

Support
Serve as a prop for, or to bear or hold up.
If you want the support of others, cast yourself as a victim. Then watch all the weak people in society, now having been given a perfect opportunity to appear strong, rush to your support. Then you will feel strong enough to return the favour, and so on.

Survival
The act or fact of surviving, particularly under adverse or unusual circumstances.
If the grocery store is suddenly empty, we can rely on the government to step in and feed us. That's taxes working for you. Sit tight, the state will provide and save us.
Also, if you feel your life might be in danger please ring the emergency services, they will always arrive on time. Or use a spoon to defend yourself. And lastly, there is always google or wikipedia.

Swedish
Relating to or originating in Sweden.
A Danish is a sweet pastry, a Kiwi is a hairy fruit, and a Swede is a vegetable, rutabaga (turnip). Being Swedish means you have evolved into passivity and are no longer prone to going berserk. Swedes are the most tolerant people on earth and are actively transforming their country into a warzone with hundreds of bombs going off every year, apparently for no obvious reason as no one wants to talk about it.

Synonym
A word with similar meaning.
A word you can use instead of the one you can't spell.

System
An organisational scheme with parts working together as an interconnecting network; a complex whole.
We have a political system and an ordering principle called democracy. It is the very best of systems, letting the majority instead of individuals decide which individuals can decide on everything in life. This system is also very popular in science where dissenting voices are drowned out and cancelled by the superior views of the collective.

7 - 30
Talk show
A radio or television show in which a host interviews or chats with guests, especially celebrity guests.
A place where important people are themselves. They can be honest and spontaneous and open up about their private lives and reveal their faux pas, flaws, foes and favourite ice cream. Nothing is ever prepared or rehearsed so it is a wonderful opportunity to learn more about the real person we look up to and to experience true and unfettered honesty from colossal idiots.

Tally
An account or reckoning; a record of debit and credit, of the score of a game, or counting bananas.
Your bar tab is a tally of achievement, your bank account is a tally of disappointment and then there is the jolly tally man who tallies the bananas.

Tantrum
A sudden and violent outburst of aggression or frustration often performed lying on the floor.
Most effectively 'thrown' by children to attain highly valued outcomes. Adults still unable to control emotional outbursts are generally found in prisons or working in professional kitchens as highly respected chefs.
See *Conniption.*

Taxation
The portion of your income you are forced to pay to the government so that they can redistribute your money according to their preferences.
This definition needs updating as every idiot knows that we are not forced to pay. Idiots everywhere willingly contribute to the state and support our politicians as they make superior choices in re-allocating our hard-earned money. However, those who don't willingly contribute should of course be thrown in jail.

A fine is a tax for doing something bad. A tax is a fine for doing something good. Either way you should be pleased to pay up as you cannot spend it as efficiently as the government can, because you are not quite as stupid as they are.

Teacher
A person who instructs.
Our first experience with authoritarianism comes from our well-meaning, but rather idiotic teacher. 'Sit down, be quiet, do as you are told'. This early training ensures that we will always be compliant little persons doing all that is expected of us. We can and do take direction and follow every sign and law without question. So much so that wearing odd socks makes us feel rebellious.

Technology
Technology is the application of scientific knowledge to the practical aims of human life or, to the change, control and manipulation of the human environment.
There are three types of technology, Communication, Medical and Mechanical. They rarely mix well with one another. Take the radio/toaster combo, electric bagpipes or clap activated bra straps for example.

Teenager
A person in their teens.
For teenagers.
Because you know what you think you know,
as a young person you are dangerously cool.
There is no more to know so let your curiosity slow,
Don't be cruel but follow the ignorant and every rule.
Know to go with the flow, there is no need to grow,
Become a pliant and proud fool, a useful adult tool.

Television
An electronic system of transmitting images with sound over a wire or wirelessly by devices that change light and sound into electrical waves and then change these back into light and sound.
Years ago, it was common to give your TV a good slap now and then. It was for its own good and it often helped. Later generations of both people and TVs have resulted in this activity becoming redundant. On reflection it may be that the latest generation may once again benefit from the occasional slap.

Tenant
A person who has the legal right to live in a particular place.
Normal wear and tear can hard to define as some tenants like abstract ventilation or confuse wallpaper with toilet paper. Being a tenant has

many advantages to being an owner, although never in the history of mankind has a tenant been successful in getting the rent lowered.
Term
A designated time period or a word or words assigned to something, like a discipline.
No matter how daft and moronic your government behaves, they are only guaranteed a term of 4 years.
The term for this is 'unbearable'.
Terrorism
Violence, unsanctioned by a government, the purpose of which is to intimidate civilian populations. Usually driven by religious, ideological or political objectives.
Terrorism is an appealing strategy for purely evil people. An idiot condemns aggressive violence of any kind. Terrorists, on the other hand, always think they are smart and know better. That is a problem.
Thankful
Feeling and expressing gratitude; appreciation.
This term will inevitably disappear within a generation as fewer and fewer young people feel they have little or anything to be thankful for. Most young people believe that catastrophic climate change and death by weather is imminent so who can blame them?
Thief
A person who steals another person's property, especially by stealth or without open force; one guilty of theft or larceny.
A term allocated to an individual engaged in unlawfully acquiring the property of another. If a group calling themselves the Mafia engages in stealing, then it is still unlawful. If the Mafia were cleverer they might change their name to "The State" (maybe some have). In this way it becomes lawful to steal, and with enough propaganda the victims of such thefts become morally convinced it is for the greater good and they willingly contribute part of every pay packet and lambast those that don't. See, and you thought you might not be an idiot.
Time
The system of sequential and indefinite relations that any event has to any other, as past, present, or future; indefinite and continuous.
Also pertaining to the temporal point as defined by hours, minutes, and seconds.
Despite the best efforts to have a common, standardized way of telling time sadly, this can never be achieved.
Sometimes time is cojoined with values, good or bad. Bad time is for instance; doing time, bedtime, or overtime, whereas good times are vacation time or time off etc.

Title
The distinguishing name of a book, poem, picture, piece of music, or the like. Or the award given to a winner in sports.
Knocking someone on their backside may earn you a title but not the kind you will find in a library. The titles within a library can number in the millions which is why you steer clear of libraries. Libraries are also staffed by delusional people who think themselves really smart, when in reality they are often more sinister and arrogantly stupid than politicians. Too many books will do that to you.

Tolerance
The capacity to endure pain or hardship, fortitude, stamina. Also, sympathy or indulgence for ideologies or actions contrasting, or conflicting with one's own.
Tolerance is a very, very important virtue. It is in fact so important that if any person disagrees with you, you should show your tolerance by silencing and ostracising them.

Totalitarianism
Absolute control of all people by a few individuals who have been given that authority by the will of the people.
Gosh. Here is an unusual new word which seems to have so much potential. A total solution. Such wonderful progress.
Many of the global elite are scrambling to assert as much power over others as possible, all thanks to the brilliant dumbing down of populations at the hands of unquestioning journalists and sycophantic bureaucrats. The world is an exciting place and being an idiot truly is a gift as the misery of it all will not even register.

Tradition
The handing down of long-established beliefs, legends, customs, information, from generation to generation, especially by word of mouth or by practice.
If elements of a minority culture is appropriated by another this is called cultural appropriation and can be very controversial. The simple solution to not offend is that we reject innovations like movies, matches and belly button lint brushes and readopt the traditional, rudimentary ways of our ancestors. In this way nobody is upset.

Train
A procession of wagons, vehicles or people moving together.
A human being is as fast as a bullet train. You just have to be on it. This means that, in the physical sense, you are no longer slow.

Training
To instruct or be instructed. Physical conditioning.

Training our bodies is very important. At least it is important to say the words. The objective of training is to look better or feel heathier. As inevitably death will follow, this 'improvement' is always temporary which makes the activity of training pretty pointless.

Transgender
A person whose gender identity does not correspond to the sex assigned at birth.
Why do people think it is acceptable to call a baby he or she? They can't speak yet so they can't say their preferred gender. Don't be transphobic, instead choose to be wholesome and respectful and call them it, or maybe just t.b.d.b.s. (to be determined by self).

Transition
Changing from one state, position, gender or subject to another.
Changing is always good. We are always evolving, and we collectively know that we always improve our situation. Nothing is getting worse. Our elected leaders will safeguard our future, our money, our health, wealth, and happiness. Changing your pronouns or even your species is also perfectly normal and can be very exciting.

Transphobic
An intense and irrational fear of, or persistent and absurd aversion to, people who claim that men can have babies and women can have penises.
Let everybody think they are normal and decide for themselves what that means. Surgical intervention can help affirm these choices. Maybe less so, at this time, for changing species, but surgical science and pharmaceuticals should soon enable us to be birds or elephants or whales. As a society we should also be free to participate in anyone else's delusions and in the name of diversity, provide funding.

Trash
Anything useless or worthless; discarded rubbish.
There is household trash and industrial trash but the term is mostly used for white trash. White trash dwells at the very bottom of the perceived evolutionary value scale which is a little unfair as they serve an important purpose. They happily and uncaringly shoulder the burden of blame for absolutely everything that is wrong with the world. Trash is only ever white. Any other colour is racist.

Travel
To journey from one place to another, as by car, train, plane, or ship; take a trip.
" Travel is the only thing you buy that makes you richer " Jonas.

Travel can also make you very poor but only if you are already poor. If you are rich, it will only make you less rich, unless you go to the Casino in Monte Carlo.

It is a familiar but idiotic concept to imagine that anywhere else, other than where you are, might be a place you would rather be. And if you would rather be there, why would you go back?

Trial
The determination of a person's guilt or innocence by due process of law.
Another word with broadening applications. A trial can now be conducted and executed by legacy media and by manufactured or popular consensus in social media. You may not be incarcerated in a prison, but the penalties are still severe and include being spat at in public and having your children ostracised and bullied in school. Better then to remain compliant and follow the collectively approved fads and trends like a good idiot.

Tribalism
Strong loyalty to one's own tribe, party, or group and extreme suspicion and disdain for the group of another.
Your self-worth as an idiot comes from joining with other idiots and belonging to the most powerful group of all; idiots. In most countries we already control the elections as we are the majority.

Trust
Reliance on the integrity, strength, ability, surety, etc., of a person or thing; confidence.
Once trust is lost it is lost for good. As we have evolved to a new level of understanding however, we now realise that those who say, "Trust me", like politicians, mean something entirely different. The word now means "Listen, I am going to lie to you, but you will believe me anyway". This is clearly demonstrated in every political election campaign.

Truth
A verified and indisputable fact, proposition, or principle.
There is no such thing as truth, all young lawyers know this. The traditional definition is sadly out of date and needs to be changed as a matter of urgency. We are proposing that the standard entry should reflect language evolution and society as a whole and read: *A verified and indisputable feeling, idea, or opinion.*

Tyranny
Unrestrained exercise of power by oppressive government or ruler.
An unfortunate description for what actually is the successful idea that a king or a dictator, a ruling oligarchy or a voting majority, always with

stated benevolent intentions benefitting the majority, expect that you will live according to their preferences, and that you also will help pay for them.
See *Democracy, Monarchy, Dictator and Stalinism.*
U - 9
Unhappiness
Sad, wretched and miserable.
The consequence of having a brain, the intensity correlating to its size, is that you will be unhappy. This is because you have an imagination and can imagine how life could be better. This is why the current trend of embracing stupidity is so rewarding; it allows us to forget what could be and embrace what is.
Give away what you have. When you have nothing, you will be content and flourish.
Union
The act of uniting two or more things, persons or states.
A Union can be memorable, like the Soviet Union and Union Carbide. Some unions improve workers' salaries through minimum wage laws and organise strikes on sunny afternoons. The unemployed can't afford a union so nobody fights the minimum wage laws that makes low end jobs disappear. But this is why we need a government, to pay money to people who don't work in jobs that aren't allowed to exist.
Universal
Applicable in all cases, everywhere.
The gradual cognitive decline, which is occurring particularly in western civilisation, is obvious and nearly universal and 'true' idiots can also recognise it, despite being immersed in it.
You might call it the last vestiges of self-awareness.
Ubiquitous
Omnipresent.
Everywhere at once, like stupidity, google or air pollution.
Unity
A whole or totality as being or combining all its parts into one.
Nobody uses this word in this context anymore except, ironically, some politicians. It now means developing games (company name) and games are not reality, which explains what the politician who says unity is doing. He or she or ze or it or they is playing a game.
Universal
Applicable everywhere or in all situations or cases. Involving or concerning all.

When the Globalists finally are in full control of this planet, they will set their sights on the rest of them.
If the movie industry can control their Universe why can't Klaus Swab control the rest?

University
The highest institution of learning.
A place where young idiots go to unlearn bad habits like thinking and reasoning and develop their brains to conform to state approved educational guidelines.
It is most important to learn about socialist income redistribution strategies, how to identify maladjusted white misogynists and how to use victimhood status and emotional arguments to avoid getting arrested when participating in nonviolent protesting like looting, burning a courthouse or supergluing yourself to a freeway.
Learning new skills to become a more effective idiot is also something that should be free of charge for all of us. It is our right to know how to be stupid.

Urges
Instinctive impulse or the act of impelling action or force.
People claim to be a victim to their own urges, like eating, but they also eat, which we all know is a voluntary activity. Uncontrollable urges are controllable but only if the will is there. Discipline is great if it comes from without, and much less reliable if it comes from within.

Utopia
An idealised world which has achieved political and social perfection.
Many millions have died in valiant attempts to attain this wonderful and well-defined goal, which we haven't yet attained. We should not let that dissuade us from further attempts. San Francisco is perhaps the best attempt so far.

V - 16

Vacant
Unoccupied, unused, empty, no contents.
Vacant seats, rooms and minds. Having a vacant mind is an unresponsive mind. This differs from stupid in that responses are slightly more predictable.

Vaccine
Any preparation injected into the body to prevent illness or disease.
Since our biology and natural immune systems fails us badly, we are fortunate that we receive between 30 and 40 injections before age 6. The fact that controlled research is conducted to create new dangerous diseases helps us develop preventative measures before those diseases are created.

Value
The subjective regard that something is held to deserve; the importance, worth, or usefulness of something as determined by an individual.
The value of anything is determined by comparing it to something else. If you rank watching TV higher than mowing the lawn then your neighbour, who ranks nice lawns higher than treating you nicely will have words with you. If you then rank watching TV higher than having a good relationship with your neighbour, then it is all on. This is how we establish what is called the hierarchy of value.

Vandalism
Deliberately and maliciously destroying or damaging property.
Vandalism of public property is sometimes done with irony or humour. If the same thing is done to private property, nobody laughs, except the occasional undertaker.

Vanity
Excessive pride in one's qualities, abilities, achievements and in particular, appearance.
There is no practical advantage in blaming the mirror but smashing it may provide temporary satisfaction.

Vegan
A vegetarian who omits all animal products from the diet, and sometimes from life.
Diesel, petrol and plastic is made from oil, which comes from dead animals. Therefore, real vegans don't drive or use any mechanical form of transport. Nor do they have elastic in their underwear or paint their walls.

Vice
Immoral or evil behaviour; or next in line.
Kamala Harris is next in line to board the school bus. The bus driver suddenly becomes unwell. What would Kamala do?

Victim
A person deceived, cheated, injured, or harmed. Also offended.
An aspirational state of being. The interpretation has recently widened to include being a victim on behalf of others. So, not only should you defend yourself and those you love. You must also defend anybody belonging to a group being victimised, even if they themselves don't realise they are victims.

All idiots know that being a victim carries with it many societal advantages so we must fight for our right to be a victim. Being a victim gives life meaning and purpose and it is both virtuous and potentially very lucrative.

Villain
An antagonist with evil intent or person causing bad outcomes like a criminal or scoundrel.
Unless you watch a Marvel movie or watch Woopie talk about conservatives, true villains are hard to come by. Most, so called villains, are actually just idiots who really don't like other idiots and then does something evil about it, like poop in their shoe.

Virtue
Conformity to moral and ethical principles. Moral excellence; goodness, and righteousness.
The highest virtue is conformity. It is the greatest achievement of strong-willed idiots to collectively subjugate ourselves to a higher purpose as guided by great leaders and superior idiots.

Violence
An unjust or unwarranted exertion of physical force or power. As against rights or laws.
"Silence is violence" we are told but speaking is also violence, say others. It is very confusing, but one thing seems very clear; if you choose violence to solve your problems and it doesn't work; then you are simply not using enough of it.

Vocabulary
A stock of words used by or known to a particular people or group of people.
Cultures are often defined by linguistic barriers but since nearly everyone can, or soon will, speak English we can look forward to programming becoming cheaper and more effective. Soon we can all share in the best of all facts and real truths of CNN.

Voluntaryism
Voluntaryism is the belief that all interaction should be voluntary and, by necessity, free of external coercion.
An illogical and frightening position much despised by the biggest idiots among us, our politicians. Voluntaryists say they haves no problems living with the fact that others, most of us, prefer a system based on forced compliance by threat of violence and incarceration. However, voluntaryists don't understand why they can't be allowed to live a life without bullying and forced coercion. Well, that is idiotic.

Voodoo
Afro-Caribbean folk magic and religion.
When karma doesn't cut the mustard, voodoo dolling might do the trick.

Voting
An expression of preference from limited alternatives, made by an individual, giving the winner of the election the moral and legal right to rule over all participants and non-participants.
A religious activity which gives everyone the opportunity to demonstrate their idiocy and to help select those politicians slightly less likely to wreck and ruin our country and impoverish us in the process. Fortunately, idiots are in majority and the majority is always right. We know best.

Vulgar
Indecent; obscene; crude; lewd.
Fun fact – crude oil, like a ballet dancer, is either heavy and sour or light and sweet.

W -20

Wage
Money received or paid in return for work or services.
You can also receive money for no work or no services and that is the actual minimum wage.
Employers are selfish of course which is why workers never get any more than the minimum wage. Why would they receive more than the law requires? Also, in the name of fairness and equity, politicians should receive the minimum wage and we feel sure they will be lowered soon.

Waiting
A period, pause, interval or delay.
Arnold memorably said "I'll be back'. The movie would not have been successful had he said "I'll wait".

War
Armed hostility, instigated and directed by individuals called ministers and generals and performed by professional soldiers.
"Death has a tendency to encourage a depressing view of war.' - Donald Rumsfeld.
Up until 100 years ago wars and battles often took place away from towns, women and children. Thankfully we are more civilised now and wars are more inclusive and will always affect civilians at least as much as soldiers.
War is also an activity that helps support the financial status of the biggest idiots of all, politicians.

Warrant
To authorize, sanction, or justify.
A search warrant is necessary for searching but it does not include a find warrant for finding or a take warrant for taking.

Wealth
A great quantity of money, property or other riches.
The greatest mystery is how wealth is created, say those who call themselves intelligent.
That is just silly. We all get our money from the government. Obviously. And they give us lots of free stuff. Every idiot always gets what we deserve. Deep inside we know this to be true. Really true.
Weapon
Any instrument or device used to defend or attack in combat.
History tells us that saying someone has weapons when they don't, can be used as a reason for attacking them (with weapons). Better then to have weapons, for a state that is, because if you are a civilian, you can trust your government to keep you safe. Civilians don't need weapons because if you find yourself in a defensive situation it is more effective to tell people in a stern voice: "I'm making a phone call"!
In extreme circumstances ordinary kitchen utensils can be used as defensive weapons but to have the desired effect, we, as idiots, need to wield them with a menacing look on our faces. Toasters, doyleys, and egg cups are ideal for this purpose.
See *Gun*
Weak
Not strong. Fragile or frail.
If a weak person is given power the results will be devastating. Never underestimate power when wielded by the frail or weak.
An idiot with power is preferrable to the weak person with power wreaking havoc on everything within reach.
Welfare
Financial or other assistance to an individual or family from a city, state, or federal government (financed by Tax and Rate payers). Also, the health and happiness of a group or individual.
This represents a small portion of the resources appropriated coercively by government to assist those in need. If the idiots in charge understood economics better, they would tax a lot more and give all of it to those in need. That way we can all live comfortably at the expensive of the rich. Forever.
Western
Located in, or toward, the west.
In reference to Western civilisation, considerable efforts are now made to remove this vast topic from many Universities. Replacing it will be socially acceptable topics such as baking science, the art of walking and how to watch television.

Whatdoyoucallit
So, not a real word yet but still synonymous with thingamajig, thingamabob, doohickie, doovadacka, doodad, gizmo, thingo and dingus.
White
The lightest of colours which is not a colour at all. It reflects all light. Opposite to black.
The colour of surrender - white flag; the colour of purity - Christianity; the colour of virginity - wedding dresses.
Viewpoint
An attitude of mind, a perspective.
There is nothing as feeble as the human mind when it is in the grip of the desire to be different, or even worse, do something creative. Conform and just go along with the rest of the idiots. It is so much more comfortable, and it certainly is consistent with human nature.
Wine
An alcoholic beverage produced from fruit, generally from grapes.
As far as relationships are concerned, few are as optimal as the one between you and wine.
Wisdom
The quality or state of being wise; knowledge of what is true or right coupled with a judicious and fair mind.
No one person is wiser than the collective. Anybody who thinks they have the right to be different in anyway is a disruptor and an antisocial antagonist and must be dealt with swiftly and forcefully. We cannot allow an individual to stand out in any way, unless of course it is a democratically elected leader which nearly always is the biggest idiot. That is different. Politicians are, by definition, more stupid than the rest of us, as demonstrated by nearly every single past leader. This should also give them special privileges, unless they are white.
Wit
"Wit is educated insolence" Aristotle.
It is, as it must be, combated, as keen perception and clever expression of ideas is nearly always regarded as offensive by the collective.
Woke
Vigilant resistance against discrimination, oppression, and injustice in your own society.
So much more than just being awake...
This is a virtuous approach and all traditional principles regarding freedom of speech, freedom of religion, freedom of movement or freedom of association can and should be quashed in our collective quest to eradicate and cancel white privilege. Male, racist, intolerant,

bigoted heterosexuals are oppressing everyone else in a systemic patriarchy imposed on the rest of us without our consent. We must not tolerate their intolerance.

Words
Utterances used to transfer opinions.
Words are ok unless they convey or invoke the truth which makes them offensive and harmful. The most effective strategy to alleviate harm is to first, collectively, ridicule the words themselves and then change their meaning and interpretation. Secondly, ridiculing the speaker is something any idiot should grow comfortable with.

Work
An exertion or effort directed to produce or accomplish something.
One should be mindful that vigorous action and work can result in a multitude of medical problems, including death, consequently work may be hazardous to your health. Stress is also a recognised contributor to heart disease which means stress and work put together can be an even more lethal combination. Fortunately, benevolent governments around the world will reward you with resources collected from other idiots which will provide for you without you having to subject yourself to the risk of working.

Worker
A person that works.
Some think that this word is synonymous with being an employee, but they are quite unrelated as you can easily do one without the being the other, and many do.
Someone who really does work will often be discriminated against because they make other workers look bad. So, if you must choose to work, the best strategy is always to only do what you need in order to fit in. The most popular and least dangerous types of work include working on your tan, your car or in a garden.
See *Job*

Writing
Characters or symbols which serve to visualise words and ideas and used to facilitate visual communication.
It is not recommended but anyone who can write can write and many do. Some think writing helps you think. But to think you write to help you think, means there is no need to write because you already think.

X-2

Xenophobia
Fear or dislike of people from other countries or of different cultures.
You have no right to fear any stranger or any guest. (Xenos – stranger or guest in ancient Greek). All guests are equally nice and respectful.

As idiots fear of strangers will thankfully be limited as it requires an active imagination, and fear not, there are many other happier things to occupy our diminishing intellects.

Xylophone
Musical instrument played with hammers.
It's like playing a piano without any fingers.
If the triangle is too easy to play or spell, try this this one.

Yellow
The colour of egg yolks, lemons and submarines.
No yolk, but laughing at the colour yellow is corny, cheesy and can drive anyone bananas.

Yes
Affirmative, assent or approval.
Yes, is sometimes no, but no is never yes.
A yes empowers you and a no defines you.

Yodel
Singing with frequent changes between the ordinary voice and falsetto, in the manner of Swiss and Tyrolean mountaineers.
This form expression has also been appropriated by random Walmart shoppers and it is predicted to become a widespread form of communication in the future.

Young
Early stage of life. Not old.
When you turn 18 you are no longer young, and you have evolved into the pinnacle of intellectual prowess, a fully grown idiot. This is evident from your extra, ordinary, cognitive abilities, your vast knowledge and profound wisdom.

Zahara
A very large desert in Africa. Possible home of an earlier civilisation.
A spelling as good as any other, embrace the new English language, boomer!

Zero
Nil.
A number representing nothing is still representing something. Why else would it be round?

Zombie
The undead creature wishing to devour you.
Young people are smart enough to be more prepared for the zombie apocalypse than the algebra test. Self-preservation trumps maths.

www.ingramcontent.com/pod-product-compliance
Lightning Source LLC
Chambersburg PA
CBHW060201050426
42446CB00013B/2939